Fisher]

RANDOLPH CALDECOTT
HIS ART AND LIFE

Randolph Caldecott was born in Chester in 1846, the son of a successful local businessman. He was head boy at the The King's School, Chester, then at the age of fifteen became a bank clerk in the village of Whitchurch in Shropshire. His leisure hours were spent in country pursuits: fishing, shooting and riding to hounds. His tall, handsome figure and charming disposition gave him a wide circle of friends. His early drawings were of banking and country life. In 1866, at the age of twenty, he moved with the bank to Manchester, where he become an evening student at the Manchester School of Art. His membership of the Brasenose Club gave him contacts in the literary and artistic world. His talent for gentle humour showed early in the work he published in local journals. In 1872 Henry Blackburn, the editor of *London Society*, persuaded Caldecott to leave his secure banking post and try his luck as a freelance artist in London. Success came quickly with commissions as London artistic correspondent for the New York *Daily Graphic, Punch, The London Graphic, Pictorial World, London Society* and *The Illustrated London News*. Invitations to illustrate books followed. A meeting with Edmund Evans, a leading colour printer, led to the partnership which produced the shilling picture books for children, which made Caldecott a household name in late Victorian and Edwardian England as 'Lord of The Nursery'.

The countryside continued to provide much of the inspiration for his work. He lived at Wybournes, Kemsing in rural Kent in the late 1870s, from where he married Marion Brind; then from 1882 at Broomfield near Frensham in Surrey. His wide circle of friends included Kate Greenaway, Walter Crane, Julia Ewing, James Whistler, George du Maurier, Thomas Armstrong, and W.L. Thomas. In 1885, with his health in decline, he was advised to try the American climate. Unfortunately Florida where he wintered experienced its worst cold spell in fifty years and he died there in February 1886. A memorial to him in St Paul's Cathedral was designed by Sir Alfred Gilbert.

In addition to his sixteen children's picture books, Caldecott illustrated *The Hartz Mountains* and *Breton Folk* by Henry Blackburn, *Old Christmas* and *Bracebridge Hall* by Washington Irving, *Poems and Songs* by Edwin Waugh, and *"Elegy on the Death of a Mad Dog"*, by Oliver Goldsmith. Many of his oil paintings, watercolours and sculptures were exhibited at the Dudley Gallery, the Fine Arts Society, The Institute of Painters in Water Colour, the Royal Manchester Institution, the Paris Salon, and the Royal Academy. His writing is as witty as his art: a collection of his letters to friends, entitled *Yours Pictorially*, was published in 1976.

Henry Blackburn, his close friend and admirer, wrote this memoir in the year of his death.

I say it is a difficult and rare virtue, to mean what we say, to love without dissimulation, to think no evil, to bear no grudge, to be free from selfishness, to be innocent and straightforward. This character of mind is something far above the generality of people; and when realized in due measure, one of the surest marks of Christ's elect.

John Henry, Cardinal Newman, *Parochial and Plain Sermons*, II, 27

ACKNOWLEDGEMENTS

We are grateful to the Board of Trustees of the Victoria and Albert Museum, London for permission to reproduce on the cover a detail of Randolph Caldecott's watercolour Returning from Church, Diana Wood's Wedding, and to Trader Horne for his photographic work.

HENRY BLACKBURN

RANDOLPH CALDECOTT

HIS ART AND LIFE

with 205 illustrations by the artist

Fisher Press

Published by Fisher Press, Post Office Box 41,
Sevenoaks, Kent TN15 6YN, England

*Randolph Caldecott: A Personal Memoir of his early Art
Career* by Henry Blackburn was first published in 1886
First published as a Fisher paperback 1995

British Library Cataloguing in Publication Data.
A catalogue record for this book is available from
The British Library

ISBN 1 874037 12 4

Printed by Antony Rowe Ltd., Chippenham, Wiltshire
Cover: Astral Printing Ltd., London

CONTENTS

THE AUTHOR

Henry Blackburn was born at Portsea in 1830 and educated at King's College, London. He was a census officer at Somerset House before becoming Private Secretary to Edward Horsman, M.P., and then a Civil Service Commisioner. In addition to his public service career he was a successful journalist, wrote travel books, and lectured on the fine arts. He was editor of *London Society* from 1870 to 1872 and edited *Academy Notes* on the artists and pictures at the Royal Academy annual exhibitions. His writings include *Life in Algeria* (1857), *Travelling in Spain* (1866), *The Pyrenees*, illustrated by Gustave Doré (1867), *Artists and Arabs* (1868), *Art in the Mountains* (1870), *The Hartz Mountains* (1871) and *Breton Folk* (1878), both illustrated by Caldecott, *The Art of Illustration* (1894) and *Artistic Travel* (1895). He did much to encourage Caldecott during his life and to perpetuate his memory after his death. Blackburn died in 1897.

LIST OF ILLUSTRATIONS.

The unpublished illustrations are marked with an asterisk *

LIST OF ILLUSTRATIONS.

APPENDIX.

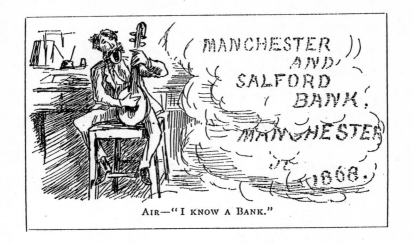

AIR—"I KNOW A BANK."

CHAPTER I.

HIS EARLY ART CAREER.

RANDOLPH CALDECOTT, the son of an accountant in Chester, was born in that city on the 22nd of March, 1846, and educated at the King's School, where he became the head boy. He was not studious in the popular sense of the word, but spent most of his leisure time in wandering in the country round. Thus, his love of sport and fondness for rural pursuits, which never forsook him, were evidenced at an early age. His artistic instincts were also early developed, and many treasured sketches, models of animals, &c., cut out of wood, were produced in Chester by the boy Caldecott.

Perhaps the best and most characteristic record of his early life is, that he and his brother were "two of the best boys in the school;" the genius that consists in "an infinite faculty for taking pains" having much to do with his after career of success.

FIRST CLERK—"GOT JONES' LEDGER?"
SECOND DO. (NEWLY MARRIED)—"YES, LOVE!"

In 1861 Caldecott was sent to a bank at Whitchurch in Shropshire, where, for six years, he seems to have had considerable leisure and opportunity for indulging in his favourite pursuits. Here, living at an old farm-house about two miles from the

town, he used to go
fishing and shooting,
to the meets of
hounds, to markets
and cattle fairs,
gathering in a store
of knowledge useful
to him in after years.
The practical, if half-
unconscious, edu-
cation that he
thus obtained in his
" off-time," as he

"Coom, then."

termed it, whilst clerk at the Whitchurch and
Ellesmere Bank, was often referred to afterwards
with pleasure. Thus from the earliest time it will
be seen that he lived in an atmosphere favourable
to his after career. But the bank work was never
neglected ; from the day he left his school in Chester
in 1861 to become a clerk in Whitchurch, until
the spring of 1872 when he left Manchester finally
for London, the record of his office work was that
he " did it well."

During the Whitchurch days he had, as we have indicated, unusual advantages of leisure, and the opportunity of visiting many an old house and farm, driving sometimes on the business of the bank, in his favourite vehicle, a country gig, and "very eagerly," writes one of his fellow clerks and intimate friends, "were those advantages enjoyed. We who knew him, can well understand how

"THREE FRIENDS."

welcome he must have been in many a cottage, farm, and hall. The handsome lad carried his own recommendation. With light brown hair falling with a ripple over his brow, blue-grey eyes shaded by long lashes, sweet and mobile mouth, tall and well-made, he joined to these physical advantages a gay good humour and a charming disposition. No wonder that he was a general favourite."

But soon he was transferred to Manchester, where a very different life awaited him—a life of more arduous duties—in the "Manchester and Salford Bank," but with opportunities for knowledge in other directions, of which he was not slow to avail himself. If in his early years his father discouraged his artistic leanings, he was now in a city which above all others encouraged the study of art—" as far as it was consistent with business." In the Brasenose Club, and at the houses of hospitable and artistic friends in Manchester, Caldecott had exceptional opportunities of seeing good work, and obtaining information on art matters.

One who knew him well at this time, writing in the *Manchester Courier* of Feb. 16th, 1886, says :—

" Caldecott used to wander about the bustling, murky streets of Manchester, sometimes finding himself in queer out-of-the-way quarters often coming across an odd character, curious bits of antiquity and the like. Whenever the chance came, he made short excursions into the adjacent country, and long walks which were never purposeless. Then he joined an artists' club and made innumerable pen and ink sketches. Whilst in this city so close was his application to the art that he loved that on several occasions he spent the whole night in drawing."

For five years, from 1867 to 1872, Caldecott worked steadily at the desk in Manchester, studying from nature whenever he had the chance in summer ; and at the school of art in the long evenings, some-times working long and late at some water colour drawing. Caldecott owed much to Manchester, as he often said, and he never forgot or undervalued the good of his early training. The friends he made then he kept always, and they were amongst his dearest and best.

In Manchester on the 3rd of July, 1868—his first drawings were published in a serio-comic paper called *Will o' the Wisp ;* and in 1869, in another paper called *The Sphinx*, he had several pages of drawings reproduced. He was painting a little at the same time, making many hunting and other studies ; they were chiefly for friends, but one picture was exhibited at the Manchester Royal Institution in 1869.

"CONSIDER, LADIES AND GENTLEMEN OF THE JURY, THE SAD POSITION IN WHICH MY CLIENT IS PLACED—DESERTED BY HIS WIFE AND LEFT TO SUPPORT HIMSELF AND TENDER INFANT BY HIS OWN EXERTIONS."

FULL CRY.

There was no restraining Caldecott now, his
artistic bent and his delightful humour were finding
expression in sketches in odd hours and minutes, on
bits of note paper, on old envelopes, and on the
blotting paper before him at his desk, until everybody about him must have been alive to his talent.
He might no doubt have eventually attained a good

"IN THE HUNTING FIELD."

position in the bank, for, as one of his friends writes
of him very truly,

"Caldecott's ability was general, not special.   It
found its natural and most agreeable outlet in art and
humour, but everybody who knew him, and those
who received his letters, saw that there were perhaps

a dozen ways in which he would have distinguished himself had he been drawn to them."

The unpublished sketches dispersed through this chapter indicate but slightly the originality and fecundity of Caldecott's genius at this time.

There was clearly but one course to pursue—to

"This is not a Culprit going to gaol—it is only a Gentleman in love who happens to be walking before a Policeman!"

give up commercial pursuits and go to London—if such sketches as these were to be found scattered amongst bank papers !

And so, in May, 1870, Caldecott, as his diary

"Society in Manchester."

records, went to London for a few days with a
letter of introduction to Mr.. Thomas Armstrong
from Mr. W. Slagg; and in the same year, 1870,
some of his drawings were shown to Shirley Brooks,
and to Mark Lemon, then editor of *Punch*.   Mr.
Clough thus records the event :—

" Bearing an introductory letter he went up to
London on a flying visit, carrying with him a
sketch on wood and a small book of drawings of
the ' Fancies of a Wedding.'   He was well received.   The sketch was accepted, and with many
compliments the book of drawings was detained.
' From that day to this,' said Mr. Caldecott, ' I
have not seen either sketch or book.'   Some time
after, on meeting Mark Lemon, the incident was
recalled, when the burly, jovial editor replied, ' My
dear   fellow,   I   am   vagabondising   to-day,   not
Punching.'   I don't think Mr. Caldecott rightly
appreciated that joke."

From this date and all through the year 1871,
Caldecott was at work in Manchester and sending to
London drawings, some of which have hardly been
exceeded for humour and expression in a few lines.

"A NEW CONTRIBUTOR."

CHAPTER II.

DRAWING FOR "LONDON SOCIETY."

It was in February 1871, in the pages of *London Society*—a magazine which at that time included amongst its contributors J. R. Planché, Shirley Brooks, Francis T. Palgrave, Frederick Locker, G. A. Sala, Edmund Yates, Percy Fitzgerald, F. C. Burnand, Arthur à Beckett, Tom Hood, Mortimer

Collins, Joseph Hatton, &c. ; and amongst its artists Sir John Gilbert, Charles Keene, Linley Sambourne, G. Bowers, Mrs. Allingham, W. Small, F. Barnard, F. W. Lawson, M.E.E., and many other notable names—that Caldecott made his first appearance before a London public.

" EDUCATION UNDER DIFFICULTIES."

On November 3rd, 1870, his diary says :—

" Some drawings which I left with A. in London have been shown, accompanied by a letter from Du Maurier, to a man on *London Society*. Must wait a bit and go on working—especially studying horses, A. said."

From this parcel of Caldecott's drawings the present writer, being the "man" referred to, selected a few to be engraved ; the sketch of the Rt. Hon.

Ye monthe of Aprile . ———

Robert Lowe on horseback in Hyde Park, on page 17, "Ye monthe of Aprile" and "Education under Difficulties" being amongst the first published.

It was suggested to him early in 1870 that he should come to London for a short time and make

sketches in Hyde Park, and it touched Caldecott's
fancy, (as he often mentioned afterwards,) that he
whose experiences were far removed from such

SKETCH IN HYDE PARK—"ROTTEN ROW."

scenes should have been chosen as a chronicler of
"Society." The sketches were made always from
his own point of view, and some were so grotesque,
and hit so hard at the aristocracy, that they were

found inappropriate to a fashionable magazine!—
one especially of Hyde Park in the afternoon,
called "Sons of Toil," had to be declined by
the Editor with real regret.

"A PASSING GLIMPSE OF A GENTLEMAN WHOM I TOOK TO BE THE
CHANCELLOR OF THE EXCHEQUER."

The packet of original sketches lies before the
writer now; the pen and ink drawing of "The
Chancellor of the Exchequer" is dated June 3rd,

C

1870. But the best and funniest of these early works could not be published in a magazine.

For Christmas time, 1871, Caldecott made many sketches. Two were to illustrate a short story called "The Two Trombones," by F. Robson, the actor.   It

"THE TROMBONE."

was a ridiculous story, bordering on broad farce, depicting the adventures of Mr. Adolphus Whiffles, a young man from the country, who in order to get behind the scenes of a theatre undertakes to act as a substitute for a friend as "one of the trombones," unknown to the leader of the orchestra.   His friend

assures him that in a crowded assembly " one trombone would probably make as much noise as two,"
and that, if he took his place in the orchestra, he had
only to " pretend to play and all would be right."

" THE TWO TROMBONES."

In the first sketch we see him in his bedroom
contemplating the unfamiliar instrument left by his
friend ; in the second he is at the theatre at the
crisis when the leader of the band calls upon him
to " play in " (as it is called) one of the performers
on to the stage !   Mr. Whiffles's instructions were

to keep his eyes on the other trombone and imitate his movements exactly; but unfortunately *the other trombone was a substitute also.* The leader looks round, and seeing the two trombones apparently perfectly ready to begin, gives the signal, and the curtain rises. The *dénoûment* may be imagined! Other stories were illustrated by Caldecott, about this period, in *London Society;* one of Indian life, another called *Crossed in Love, &c.,* but the artist wished that some illustrations should not be reprinted. Several drawings from *London Society* are omitted, from the same cause.

CHRISTMAS DAY, 4.30 A.M.
"PLEASE, SIR, GIVE ME A CHRIST-
MAS-BOX."

The freshness of fancy, not to say recklessness of style, in many of the drawings which came by post at this time—the abundance of the flow from a stream, the course of which was not yet clearly

"CLINCHING AN ARGUMENT." SKETCH AT A "DEBATING AND MUTUAL IMPROVEMENT SOCIETY."

marked—raised embarrassing thoughts in an editor's mind. " What to do with all the material sent ? " was the question in 1871—a question which Caldecott was soon able to answer for himself.

In 1871, many favourable notices appeared in the press referring to the humorous illustrations in *London Society;* but the sketch of all others

" SNOWBALLS."

which attracted attention to the work of the unknown artist was " A Debating and Mutual Improvement Society" on page 21, a recollection probably of some meeting or actual scene in Manchester.[1] Here the artist was on his own ground,

---

[1] The drawing, *A Debating Society*, was very well engraved on wood by J. D. Cooper, and appeared in *London Society* in 1871, v. xx. p. 417 ; it is now reproduced on a larger scale by a mechanical process of photo-engraving. Experts in drawing for book illustration may be interested to compare results.

"HEIGH-HO, THE HOLLY!"

*　　*　　*　　*

" That's not Rosalind : oh dear no—
　That damsel under the misletoe,
　　Who seems to think life jolly :
　And as to the gentleman there behind,
　He wouldn't have pluck to kiss Rosalind,
　　Can't you fancy his 'Heigh-ho, the Holly !'"

MORTIMER COLLINS.

and the result is one of the most rapid and spontaneous sketches in pen and ink ever achieved. It
had many of the characteristics of his later work,
a lively and searching analysis of character, without
one touch of grossness or ill-nature—fun and satire
of the subtlest and the kindliest. Here was the
touch of genius unmistakable, an example of
expression in line seldom equalled.

In an altogether different vein, drawing with pen,
and a brush for the tint,—the new artist tries his
hand at illustrating one of Mortimer Collins's
madrigals called " Heigh-ho, the Holly!"

Amongst the most ambitious and interesting of
Caldecott's drawings at this time were his "hunting
and shooting friezes," of which several examples will
be found in the pages of *London Society* for 1871
and 1872, drawn in outline with a pen; showing,
thus early, much decorative feeling and a liking for
design in relief which never left him in after years.

Two of the best that he did were the hunting
subjects, entitled "Going to Cover" and "Full
Cry."

" The Coming of Age of the Pride of the Family "

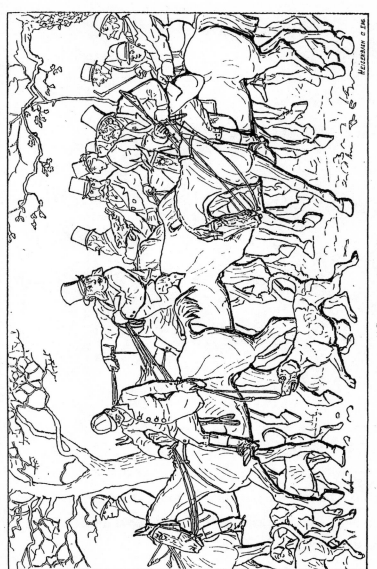

"Going to Cover."

HEIDENBACH G. ENG.

is another example, in a different style, of Caldecott's drawing in line at this period. It is reproduced opposite, in exact facsimile from the pen and ink drawing in possession of the writer.

HYDE PARK—"OUT OF THE SEASON."

Trivial as these things may seem now, the arrival in Manchester of the red covers of *London Society* containing almost every month something new by R. C., were among the events in the life of the young banker's clerk which soon set the tide of his affairs towards London.

"Coming of Age of the Pride of the Family."

Referring to drawings made for the magazine after Midsummer 1872, when Mrs. Ross Church succeeded to the editorship, Caldecott writes to a friend :—

" Florence Marryat wants me to illustrate a novelette very humorous, to run through five or six numbers of *London Society*, beginning in February. Engraved illustrations, no ' process.' I think I shall do them, I want coin ! "

But he had soon other work in hand as will be seen in the next chapter.

"THE END OF ALL THINGS."

SKETCH ON A POST CARD.

CHAPTER III.

IN LONDON, THE HARZ MOUNTAINS, ETC.

EARLY in the year 1872 Caldecott left Manchester for London, "bearing with him the well wishes of the Brazenose Club and of an extensive circle of friends." This great change was not decided upon without considerable hesitation; but, to quote again from a Manchester letter :—

"Caldecott was greatly encouraged to take this step by the sale of some small oil and water colour paintings at modest prices, and by the acceptance of drawings by London periodicals. The clinking of sovereigns and the rustling of bank-notes became sounds of the past—the fainter the pleasanter, so at least Caldecott thought at that time, with energy, ardour, and the world before him."

In February and March, 1872, he was still drawing for the magazines and illustrating short stories.

In March, 1872, he exhibited hunting sketches in oil at the Royal Institution, Manchester.

On the 16th April he went to the Slade School to attend the Life Class under E. J. Poynter, R.A., until the 29th June.

As this was the turning point in Caldecott's career, it should be recorded that at this time, and ever afterwards, Mr. Armstrong, the present Art Director at the South Kensington Museum, was his best friend and counsellor.[1]   He had also the advantage of the friendship of George du Maurier, M. Dalou, the sculptor, Charles Keene, Albert Moore, and others.

On the 8th June he records, " A. urged me to prepare caricatures of people well known," probably with the view of making drawings for periodicals.

---

[1] In a private letter to the writer of this memoir, dated 2nd November, 1876, Caldecott says :—" Pen can never put down how much I owe, in many ways, to T. A."

Several drawings of Caldecott's were under consideration by the proprietors of *Punch*, and on the 22nd June, 1872, the first appeared.

In the same month he exhibited a frame of four small sepia drawings at the Black and White Exhibition, Egyptian Hall, London.

FIRST DRAWING IN "PUNCH," 22ND JUNE, 1872.

On the 28th June his diary records, " in the gallery of the House of Commons attending the debate on the Ballot Bill ; " and again on the 8th July. On the 9th he is " engaged on chalk caricatures all day."

A letter dated 21st July, 1872, to one of his Manchester friends is worth having for the ludicrous sketch accompanying it.　He writes : —

"London is of course the proper place for a young man, for seeing the manners and customs of society, and for getting a living in some of the

"A COOL SEQUESTERED SPOT."

less frequented grooves of human labour, but for a residence give me a rural or marine retreat. I sigh for some 'cool sequestered spot, the world forgetting, by the world forgot.'

About this time it was suggested to him to illustrate a book of summer travel, and on the 20th August 1872 he enters in his diary :—

"To Rotterdam, Harzburg, &c., to join Mr. and Mrs. B. in the *Harz Mountains.*"

This was the first book that Caldecott illustrated ; [1]

---

[1] *The Harz Mountains, a Tour in the Toy Country,* by Henry Blackburn.

"A Tour in the Toy Country."

D

the title suggested was "*A Tour in the Toy Country*," and before leaving London he made the drawing on the preceding page.

Caldecott, being then twenty-six, started on this journey with great readiness. The idea was altogether delightful to him; and here, as in every country he visited in after years, his playful fancy

A MOUNTAIN "BEER GARDEN."

and facility for seizing the grotesque side of things stood him in good stead.

In a strange land, amidst unfamiliar scenes and faces, he roamed "fancy free"; in a country so compact in size that the whole could be traversed in a month's walking tour.

With *Baedeker's Guide* (English edition) in his pocket, and a dialogue book of sentences in

German and English, he used
to delight to interrogate the
wondering natives ; the necessary questions difficult to find,
and "the elaborate and quite
unnecessary " (as he expressed
it), always turning up.   Such

A " FRAULEIN."

little incidents gave opportunity to the observant
artist to study the faces of the listeners ; the inter-
views conducted slowly and gravely, and ending in
a peal of laughter from the natives.

A MOUNTAIN PATH.

Life at a German watering-place, as seen on a small scale in summer in the Harz mountains, was Caldecott's first experience of scenes with which his

A WARRIOR OF SEDAN IN A BEER GARDEN AT GOSLAR, 1872.

name afterwards became familiar in the pages of the *Graphic* newspaper. In looking ·at these early sketches we must bear in mind that they were made at a time when Caldecott, as an "artist," was scarcely two years old; that although his sense of humour was overflowing, his hand was comparatively untrained; that with his keen eye for the grotesque he turned his back upon much that was beautiful about him, that his sense of the fitness of things, of the requirements of composition and the like, were in embryo, so to speak.

Nevertheless, as indicated in the next few pages,

he has left us work which, if ever a more complete
life of Caldecott should be written, would form
an important chapter in his art career.

Although little fitted for a mountaineer, he could
not resist excursions to the highest points, and with
a will which surmounted all difficulties, reached one
evening the summit of the famous "Brocken."
What he saw is recorded in the sketch below.

"THE ARK OF REFUGE."

There is a legend that when the deluge blotted
out man from most parts of the earth, the waters of
the northern seas penetrated far into Germany, and
that the enormous rock which forms the top of
the Brocken formed a shelter and resting-place.

There was no need of a romantic legend to
suggest to the mind, at the first sight of the
primitive hostelry on the top of the Brocken, its

similitude to the " ark of refuge." The situation was delightful ; we were in the "toy country" without doubt. There was the identical form of packing-case which the religious world has with one consent provided as a plaything for children ; there were Noah and his family, people walking two and two, and horses sheep, pigs, and goats stowed away at the great side door.

The resemblance was irresistible, and more attractive to Caldecott's mind than any of the legends and mysteries with which German imagination has peopled the district.

There is " no holding" Caldecott now ; on the

THE DANCE OF WITCHES.

" Hexen Tanzplatz," the sacred ground of Goethe's
poetic fancy, within sound almost of the songs of
the spirit world that haunt this lonely summit, he
sets to work.

"SPECTRES OF THE BROCKEN."

The dance of witches, so weird and terrible, (as
lately seen on the Lyceum stage in Henry Irving's
production of *Faust*,) took a different form in the
young artist's eyes, whose fancy sketch from the
Hexen Tanzplatz is reproduced opposite.   He had
been properly " posted," as he expressed it, he had

read all that should be read about ghosts, witches, and
spectres, and the result is before us. The last sketch

A SKETCH AT SUPPER.

from the dreary sum-
mit, showing the
patient tourists wait-
ing to see the view,
was all we could get
from him of spectres
of the Brocken.

One or two sketches
of the interior of his
Noah's ark, when some sixty travellers had as-
sembled to supper, completed his subjects.

It may be noted that the feeling for landscape
which Caldecott possessed in after years in such a

"BACK TO THE VIEW."

high degree, if it touched him here, was not recorded in pencil.   The magnificent scenery eastward
through the valley of the
River Bode, the grim iron
foundries and ochre mines,
and the wonderful view
from the heights above
Blankenberg, familiar to
all travellers in the Harz,
was recorded in only two
sketches; one of a roadside
inn, where we were invited
to stay, the other of two
tourists *en route.*

THE GUIDE AT GOSLAR.

How, at the little wayside sheds and "drink
gardens" scattered on the mountain paths, the tourists
sat persistently back to the view which they had
toiled miles to see, were depicted by the artist in
pencil, and many little incidents on the road were
dotted down for future use.

In the old tenth-century city of Goslar, Caldecott's
pencil was never at rest.   Taking a guide to save
time (whose portrait he gives us, with a note of a

curious sixteenth-century street door) he explores
from morning to night, choosing as subjects always
"the life of the place."

PROCESSION OF THE SICK.

" Drinking the waters
at Goslar" in 1872 was a
crude effort artistically,
which may be contrasted
with his sketches of the
same scenes at Buxton in
1876, but the humour is
irresistible. An extract
from our diaries is necessary here to explain the
illustration.

" The figures are pilgrims, that have come from far
and wide to combine the attractions of a summer
holiday with the benefits of a wonderful ' cure ' for
which the city is celebrated. The promenades and
walks on the ramparts lined with trees, are going
through the routine of getting up early, taking regu-
lar exercise and drinking daily several pints of a
dark mixture having the appearance, taste, and effect
of taraxacum or senna. The bottles are supplied at
the public gardens and cafés situated at convenient
distances in the suburbs of Goslar."

DRINKING THE WATERS AT GOSLAR.

On another day he encounters a school starting
for two or three days on the mountains, the band
making hideous noises as the procession passes out
of Goslar. Everything is characteristic here and full
of local colour ; the order of march, the costumes

A GENERAL IN THE PRUSSIAN ARMY.

and the boots of the
boys, and the general
gravity of the com-
pany are given ex-
actly — making the
usual allowance for
exaggeration. In the
background is seen
one of the iron fac-
tories and an indication of a bit of Harz scenery ;
the sketch recalling the incident with wonderful
vraisemblance. The "School on the March" in
its humour and exaggeration may remind the
reader of some drawings by Thackeray.

Here, as in Belgium, the harnessing of dogs to
carts, drawing sometimes two people over the rough
cobble stones of Goslar, excited Caldecott's pity and
anger ; he made several sketches of the animals and

"A SCHOOL ON THE MARCH"—HARZ MOUNTAINS, 1872.

one portrait of their master who had just got down
to enjoy a pipe at the corner of a street.

Sketches at
various *table
d'hôtes* in hotels,
public gardens
and the like,
were plentiful
and perpetual.
But the ma-
jority were de-
stroyed or put
away ; out of
fifty only one
such as "A
General in the Prussian Army" (see page 44)
being selected for reproduction.[1]

At Clausthal we joined a party to explore one of
the iron mines, and Caldecott gives a sketch of the

---

[1] This, and other similar sketches, caused amusement in some circles and
offence in others, at Berlin, where it was stated erroneously that the artist had
caricatured some well-known personages who came annually to Goslar to drink
the waters, and an arrangement to publish a translation of the *Harz Mountains*
into German fell through in consequence.

preparations. A note from our diary will best explain the situation.

"In order to descend the mines at Clausthal, visitors have to divest themselves of their ordinary costumes and put on some cast-off suits of ill-fitting garments left at the entrance to the mine for the purpose. As we approach the mouth of the shaft where the miners are waiting with lanterns to commence the descent, our party,—consisting of four Englishmen—a professor of geology, a director of mines, an editor and an artist—present the somewhat undignified aspect in the sketch. This change of costume is necessary on account of the wet state of the mines, the thick caps being a protection against loose pieces of ore and the wet earth that falls from time to time in the galleries."

Caldecott gives the generally dismal and disreputable appearance of the party with great verve ; his own portrait is presented in a few touches in the background, hurrying into garments much too big for him.

On one occasion the artist takes a solitary walk between Thale and Clausthal, a pathway lined in

some parts by rows of
trees with forbidden fruit,
a novel and tempting ex-
perience. There being no
mention of this route in
the guide books, he writes
as he says his " own
Baedeker " in the familiar
practical manner :—

" I start at 3.40 P.M. from the ' Tenpounds Hotel '
at Thale to walk up the valley of the Bode, over a
wooden bridge, then through a beer garden, round a
rocky corner," &c. " The way next through woods
of beech, birch and oak ; a stream can be heard but
not seen.   Treseburg is reached at 5.40 ; a prettily
situated village by the water side ; homely inn, damp
beds."

" Leave Treseburg at 9.40 A.M. over a bridge on
the right bank of the Bode.   Altenbrack at 10.50,
Wendefurth at 11.50.   Rubeland reached at 2.30 P.M.,
and so on to Elbingerode, where a halt is made for
the night at the ' Blauer Engel,' a tolerable inn.
Women of burden and foresters are the only
wayfarers met with.

" The route hence south-west over high open

land with fine views to the iron works of Rothehütte
in an hour.   Thence up a hill for half an hour and
through dense fir woods, then out on the high road
again, resting at the ' Brauner Hirsch ' at Braunlage.
From thence over hills commanding a vast extent
of country with the familiar form of the Brocken
continually in view.   The road descends by easy
stages through a district full of small reservoirs and
leads the traveller in about two hours into the wide,
clean, empty streets of Clausthal."

On the 19th September,
1872, Caldecott is at work
again in his rooms at 46,
Great Russell Street (opposite
the British Museum) arranging
with the writer for some of his
Harz Mountain drawings to
accompany an article in the
London *Graphic* newspaper.
These appeared in the autumn
of 1872.

AT CLAUSTHAL.

On the 18th October, the following entry appears
in Caldecott's diary : " Called at *Graphic* office,
saw Mr. W. L. Thomas, who took my address."

This entry is interesting as the beginning of a long connection with the *Graphic* newspaper which proved mutually advantageous.

In November, 1872, the present writer went to America, taking a scrap-book of proofs of the best of Caldecott's early drawings, a few of which were published in an article on the *Harz Mountains* in *Harper's Monthly Magazine* in the spring of 1873.[1] His drawings were also shown to the conductors of the *Daily Graphic*, of New York, which led to an engagement referred to in the next chapter.

During the latter part of 1872 numerous small illustrations were produced for *London Society*.

---

[1] Amongst the young artists in the art department of *Harper's Magazine* in 1873, was E. A. Abbey, the well-known illustrator of old English subjects; in later years a great friend and ally of Caldecott.

SKETCH IN "PUNCH," 8TH MARCH, 1873.

CHAPTER IV.

DRAWING FOR "THE DAILY GRAPHIC."

SOME idea of the work on which Caldecott was engaged in 1873 and 1874, may be gathered from extracts from his diary in those years. They are interesting if only to show that at that early period his art studies were varied, and that his experience was not confined to book illustration as has generally been supposed.

In January, 1873, he made six illustrations for
Frank Mildmay by " Florence Marryatt," and on
January 22nd, an " Initial for *Punch*."

In February—

" Began wax-modelling for practice, hearing
that my hunting frieze (white on brown paper)
had been successful in Manchester, and that I
should perhaps be asked to model some animals
for a chimney-piece."

24th April.—" A. came to see my wax models ;
liked them, said I must do something further."

Several hunting subjects were also in progress at
this time. Next are two letters to a friend in
Manchester.

"46, GREAT RUSSELL STREET, LONDON, W.C.,
"*March* 28, 1873.

" MY DEAR——,—The ancient Romans said, or
ought to have said, that ingratitude was the greatest
of human crimes. But, my dear fellow, I am not
an ingrate. I have not forgotten you—unless, as
the poet sings, ' if to think of thee by day and
dream of thee by night, be forgetting thee, thou
art indeed forgot.' I did receive your last collected joke, and a very good joke it was—for a
Manchester joke. I'm sorry that I have not power
to use it, but it will keep, although it will tread
on some people's feelings when used. The fact

A CHECK.

is that this same joke nearly brought me to an
untimely end. I went out hunting on the day I
received it, and at one fence and ditch I had quite
enough to do to avoid a rabbit-hole on the taking-
off side and some barked boughs of fallen timber
on the landing side—not to mention some low-
hanging oak trees. Well, just when I was in the
air I thought of your joke and smiled all down one
side ; my hunter—by King Tom, out of Blazeaway's
dam, by Boanerges — took the opportunity of
stumbling, and, before an adult with all his teeth
could get as far as the third syllable in 'Jack
Robinson,' my nose was engaged in cutting a
furrow all across a fine grass field, some eight acres
and a half in extent, laid down after fine crops of
seeds and roots, and well boned last winter. However, in less than half a minute (having retained
possession of the reins), I was again chasing the
flying hounds.

"About the middle of February I went down into
the country to make some studies and sketches,
and remained more than a month. Had several
smart attacks on my heart, a little wounded once,
causing that machine to go up and down like a
lamb's tail when its owner is partaking of the
nourishment provided by a bounteous Nature.
Further particulars in our next—no more paper
now. I hope you and —— are well, and with kind
regards, remain yours faithfully,

"R. C."

"46, GREAT RUSSELL STREET, LONDON, W.C.,
"*April* 27, 1873.

" MY DEAR——,—I was delighted to receive your letter—quite a long one for you.   I hope that you had a fine time of it at the ball.   Dancing is not absolutely necessary to a man's welfare temporally or spiritually;   so if you be a 'Wobbler,' wobble away and fear not, but see that thou wobblest with all thy might, then shall thy zeal compensate for lack of skill.   I've nearly given up gymnastics. I only danced twenty-one times at the last ball.

*   *   *

" I now find that during quadrilles my mind wanders away from the subject before it, and I am continually reminded that I ought to be idiotically squaring away at some one instead of cogitating with my noble back leaning against the wall. 'Sed tempora new potater,' &c. I hope you are all well, and with kind regards, remain yours faithfully,

                                        "R. C."

In May he is "working in clay in low relief."

6th June.—"Began modelling mare and foal in round."

In the latter part of June, and in July, he is "at Vienna with Mr. Blackburn," engaged on various illustrations for the *Daily Graphic*.

It was in the summer of 1873 that it occurred to the proprietors of the *Daily Graphic* (the American illustrated newspaper referred to) that the Gulf Stream, and the strong prevailing current of wind easterly from the continent of America in that latitude, might be turned to profitable account for advertising purposes. They constructed a large balloon which hung high above the houses in Broadway for some weeks, and announced that on a certain day the *Daily Graphic* balloon would sail for Europe. The start was telegraphed to London and gravely announced in the *Times* and other London papers, and every one was on the *qui vive* for this new arrival in the air.

The humour and absurdity of the situation was

"LOOKING OUT FOR THE 'GRAPHIC' BALLOON."

seized at once by the comic journals, but probably nothing that appeared at the time was more telling than the drawing made by Caldecott at Farnham

Royal for the *Daily Graphic*, and published in New York as a page of that newspaper.

Other drawings followed, descriptive of various scenes in London and England, such as a special service by Cardinal Manning at the Pro-Cathedral in Kensington; an address by Bradlaugh at the east end of London; a London picture exhibition; hunting in a northern county, &c., and Caldecott, to whom all this was a new experience, was pleased to work for the American newspaper as " London artistic correspondent."

In this capacity Caldecott went with the writer to Vienna to the International Exhibition of 1873, and there were sent to America various satirical sketches, accompanying letters, notably one of the banquet held on the 4th of July, with portraits of some well-known American citizens. One of the most successful and life-like of the smaller sketches was a Vienna horse-car entitled—" Off to the Exhibition," reproduced here.

The experience gained in various excursions during Caldecott's engagement with the *Daily Graphic*, was most valuable to him in after years ;

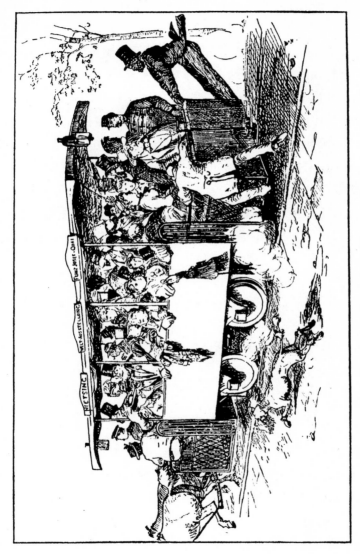

Off to the Exhibition—Vienna, 1873.

although as we have elsewhere said, illustrated
journalism properly so-called, was never sympathetic
to him, nor would his health have been equal to the
strain of so trying an occupation. As *occasional*
contributor to an illustrated newspaper he was
destined to be without a rival, as the columns of the
London *Graphic* for many years have testified.

The humour and vivacity, the *abandon*, so to
speak, exhibited in some of these early drawings,
form a delightful episode in his early art career,

A VIENNESE DOG.

and many will wonder, looking at the variety of
movement and expression (in the drawing of the
overloaded car, for instance), that the artist should
have been amongst us so long without more
recognition. It is true that his drawings were

uncertain, and that the results of want of training were sometimes too palpable ; that the accusa-
tion made in 1872 that the editor of *London Society*
had chosen " an artist who could not draw a lady,"
could hardly be gainsaid in 1873.

The artistic interest in these drawings is great,
if only from the fact that they are amongst
the few of his works drawn in pen and ink for
direct reproduction without the intervention of the
wood-engraver. Caldecott was one of the first
to try, and to avail himself of, the various
methods of reproduction for the newspaper press ;
and in the pages of the *Daily Graphic*, his facile
touch and play of line was made to appear
with startling emphasis on the printed page.[1]

But after all, the humour and drollery of
Caldecott's nature appears with more unrestrained
effect in the sketches on his letters to friends, such
as are scattered through this volume ; the natural
awe of publication in any form having a restraining
effect.

---

[1] The drawings in the *Daily Graphic* in New York were all reproduced by
photo-lithography, and printed at the lithographic press.

In July and August he is working "in the loose box at Farnham Royal," the country cottage sketched on page 90 and referred to in the following and other letters.

"HOGARTH CLUB, 84, CHARLOTTE STREET, FITZROY SQUARE, W.

"DEAR——,—The poet sings, 'Oh! have you seen her lately?' to which I answer, 'Yes.' But, whether or no, I returned to-day from a fortnight's sojourn in Buckinghamshire, and the first thing I was going to do was to write to you and say that I have no acquaintance with the happy medium who resides in my very old rooms in Great Russell Street. I have left those rooms, and am a wanderer and an Ishmaelite. I dare not take those rooms when she leaves. I called at the house just now and found another note from you. I had a good look at Europe during my Vienna expedition. I

was away a month and saw many towns, and con-
versed with many peoples and tongues.   I could
say much, but will defer till we meet over the
flowing bowl.   Since I came back I have been
staying with a friend at Holborn Circus, and also
with some friends at Farnham Royal, near Slough,
a lovely country place.   There I have been working
off some sketches of Vienna and England for the
use of the neighbouring country of America.   But
I could not help being interrupted.   Fancy a being
like this bobbing about!   Howsomedever, I am
again in town at Bank Chambers, Holborn Circus,
E.C., where I may be consulted daily.   Please
observe signature on the box, without which none
others are genuine, post free for thirteen stamps.
So you see that I have had a seven weeks' delightful
mixture of toil and pleasure, and ought now to have
a bout of toil only.   There is a book waiting to be
illustrated.

"R. C."

In the same month (August 1873), he went with
a letter of introduction to Dalou, the French sculptor,
then living in Chelsea.   Of this interview he writes,
" M. Dalou very kind in hints, showing me clay,
&c."   A friendship followed, cemented in the first

instance by a bargain that Caldecott should come
and work at the studio and teach the sculptor
to talk English, whilst Dalou helped him in his
modelling! Caldecott profited by the arrangement,
and often spoke in after years of the value of

EARLY DECORATIVE DESIGN, THE PROPERTY OF G. AITCHISON, A.R.A.

Dalou's practical teaching.   Many visits were paid
to the sculptor's studio in the year 1873.

In the intervals of work Caldecott also made
life studies at the Zoological Gardens in London,
and anatomical studies of birds.

In September he made a drawing of Mark Twain lecturing in London, for the *Daily Graphic*, and in October records the purchase by Mr. G. Aitchison, the architect, of a cast of his "first bas relief," a hunting subject; also of "two brown paper pelican drawings," one reproduced on the last page.

In November he writes the following to a friend in Manchester :—

"46, GREAT RUSSELL STREET, W.C.,
"*November* 16, 1873.

"DEAR——,—I have nothing to say to you— nothing at all. Therefore I write. I don't like writing when I have aught to say, because I never feel quite eloquent enough to put the business in the proper light for all parties. Having a love and yearning for Bowdon and Dunham, and the 'publics' which there adjacent lie, I think of you on these calm Sunday evenings about the hour when my errant legs used to repose beneath the deal of the sequestered inn at Bollington. How are you? I was pleased to see that the *Athenæum* gave a long space to your book, although I presume you did not care for the way they reviewed it. That is nothing. I have been very busy—not coining money, oh no!—but occupied, or I should say have descended into the country, during last month.

' Graced with some merit, and with more effrontery ;
his country's pride, he went down to the country.'
My summer rambles shall be talked of, and the
wonderful works in the regions of art shall be
described when next I see you.   Till then, farewell !
This short letter is like a call.—Yours, R. C."

The last entry of interest in his diary in 1873, is
on December 3rd.

"To *Graphic* office, saw Mr. Thomas.   Fixed
that I should go down to Leicestershire next week
for hunting subjects."

"THIS IS NOT A FIRST-CLASS COW."

STUDIES FOR A LARGE DECORATIVE DESIGN, 1874.

CHAPTER V.

DRAWING FOR "THE PICTORIAL WORLD," ETC.

LET us now glance at Caldecott's diary for 1874, which, with his letters to friends and the sketches which so often accompanied them, give an insight into the character of his work at this time. It is altogether an extraordinary record.

On the 14th of January, 1874, he is "working in the afternoons, sketching swans at Armstrong's." This was part of a large decorative design which he afterwards assisted in painting (see illustration on page 89).

On the 23rd January, 1874, is an interesting note.

" J. Cooper, engraver, came and proposed to illustrate, with seventy or eighty sketches, Washington Irving's *Sketch Book.* Went all through it and left me to consider. I like the idea."

In February he completed a drawing of the Quorn Hunt for the *Graphic* newspaper.

On the 12th March, he enters in his diary, " Preparing sketch of choir for W. Irving's *Sketch Book ;*" showing that he was already at work on the book which was to make his reputation.

At the same time he was preparing illustrations and trying new processes of drawing for reproduction, to aid in founding a new newspaper.

How far Mr. Caldecott was ready to conquer difficulties in his art, and how heartily he aided his friends in any project with which he was connected, are matters of history closely connected with his engagement on the *Pictorial World,* which had a bright promise for the future in 1874.

Some of the large illustrations were produced by Dawson's " Typographic Etching " process. The drawings were made with a point on plates covered with a thin coating of wax, the artist's needle, as in etching, removing the wax and exposing the surface of the plate wherever a line was required in relief—"a fiendish process!" as Caldecott described it, but with which he succeeded in obtaining excellent results—better than any artist previously.

On the 7th of . March, 1874, a new illustrated newspaper called the *Pictorial World* was started in London, of which the present writer was the art editor.

It was the time of the general election of 1874, when the defeat of Mr. Gladstone, the question of " Home Rule," and many exciting events were being recorded in the newspapers. Caldecott was asked to make a cartoon of the elections, and at once sat down and made the pencil sketch overleaf.

For some reason this drawing was not completed ; but instead, a group of various election scenes was drawn by him and appeared in the *Pictorial World*.

There were numerous sketches combined on one page, three of which are reproduced here. The illustrations on pages 70, 72, 80, 81, 82, and 84 were drawn (generally under great pressure of

THE POLLING BOOTH.

time) with an etching needle on Dawson's plates. This was the beginning of what are now familiarly known as " process " drawings in newspapers, but the system of photographic engraving, now largely used, was not then perfected. In 1874 it would have been impossible to reproduce rapidly in a newspaper, either the delicate lines of a pen and

HOME RULE—MARCH 1874.
Facsimile of pencil sketch for the *Pictorial World.*

ink sketch, or such a pencil drawing as that given above.

Caldecott rendered valuable assistance at this time, and the early numbers of the paper are

worth having if only for the reproduction of his
work.   It is not generally known how many of the
large illustrations in the *Pictorial World* were by

"ON THE STUMP."

his hand, or how much he was identified with the
publication in the first days of its career.

Amongst the best illustrations by Caldecott for
the newspaper at that period were sketches and

studies that he had made for pictures, selected from his studio; such for instance as " Coursing," " Somebody's Coming," and the " Morning Walk," on pp. 75, 77, and 86. The latter design was

THE SCOTCH ELECTIONS—"GOING TO THE HUSTINGS."

not drawn specially for the *Pictorial World*, but Caldecott made a drawing of it for the paper, which appeared in the number for 18th July, 1874.

From a bundle of sketches (some very pretty) of subjects connected with Saint Valentine, he

made a page for the same paper. These again, may
seem small matters to record, but they are facts
in the history of a life teeming with interest,

PAIRING
TIME.

and show that Caldecott's talent as an illustrator
was revealed in 1874; that he was "invented," as
the saying is, long before the publication of
Washington Irving's *Sketch Book.*

COURSING.

On the 31st of October, 1874, Mr. Henry Irving made his first appearance in London as Hamlet, one of those occasions on which the theatre was crowded with critics and well-known personages. Caldecott, altogether inexperienced in such work, made several rough sketches, seizing the grotesque side "as far as he dared" as he said.

The trying nature of that performance, and the flitting about on the stage of the nervous anxious

A VALENTINE.

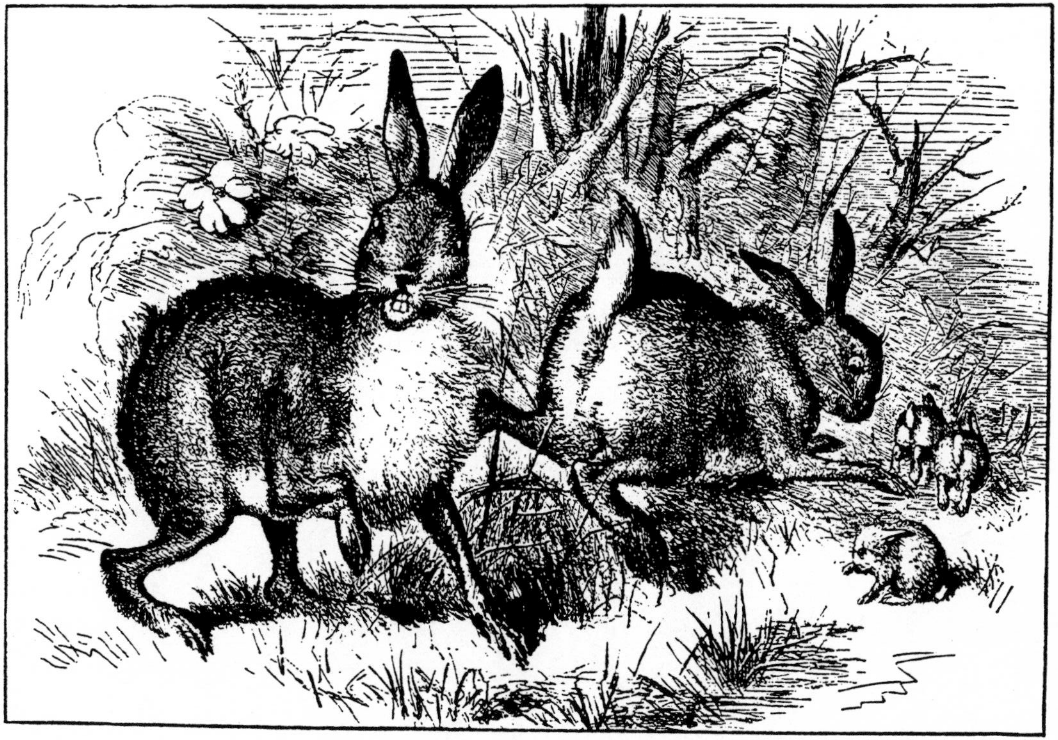

"Somebody's Coming!"

figure, with the ever-present white pocket-handker-
chief in his belt—will be remembered by many.
Caldecott made the best sketch that he could

from the left side of the dress-circle, the only
position in the house that could be obtained for him.

In company with the writer, Caldecott made
various sketches in the House of Commons, the
Law Courts, the theatres, and the like. The first
three sketches of the House of Commons—one
showing " The Arrival of the New Members,"

another, "The Speaker going up to the Lords,"
and a third, "At the Bar of the House of Lords"
—were amongst the funniest of the series. Others
followed from week to week, such as "The new

"THE YOUNG HAMLET."

Prime Minister," on page 83. On one occasion he
went down to Westminster Hall to see the Rt. Hon.
Benjamin D'Israeli enter the House of Commons

HOUSE OF COMMONS, MARCH 1874—ARRIVAL OF NEW MEMBERS.

as the *new prime minister*, and to a large illustration showing the north door of Westminster Hall (the architecture drawn by Mr. Jellicoe), he added the

" THE SPEAKER GOING UP TO THE LORDS."

figures, a grotesque group of bystanders, presumably Conservatives, welcoming their new representative. (See the *Pictorial World*, March 7th, 1874.)

It was an exciting time politically and socially, and many events of interest had to be recorded.

"AT THE BAR OF THE HOUSE OF LORDS."

Amongst them the conclusion, amidst general rejoicing, of the great Tichborne Trial on March 2nd, 1874, a trial which had lasted 188 days.

This was an opportunity for the artist. Caldecott's original sketch of this subject, if it is in existence, should be treasured ; some idea of the humour of it may be gathered from the drawing overleaf which

"THE NEW PRIME MINISTER."

was crowded into the corner of the newspaper. He also made a highly grotesque and artistic model in terra-cotta of the Tichborne Trial, now in the possession of Mr. Stanley Baldwin of Manchester.

About this time, Caldecott went to the " farewell benefit" of the late Benjamin Webster and sketched the actor—surrounded by members of his company —making his final bow to the public.

THE TICHBORNE TRIAL—"BREAKING-UP DAY."

On the eighteenth birthday, the "coming of age," of the late Prince Imperial of France, Caldecott went to Chislehurst.   The drawing of the crowd on the lawn of Camden House in a state of general congratulation, the ceremony of presentation of enormous bouquets of violets and the like; of Frenchmen and their wives, of diplomatists, and others, will be found in the *Pictorial World* for March 21st, 1874.

Here was a comparatively unknown artist at work, revealing talent which in after years would delight the world.

But fortunately for his health and peace of mind, and also for his future career, the young artist, who two years before had given up a clerkship in a Manchester bank (a "certainty" of more than £100 a year), was advised to refuse an engagement on the *Pictorial World* of £10 10s. a week, which, had it been carried out, would have done much to raise the fortunes of that newspaper.

But the rush and hurry of journalistic work was distasteful to him; he had many commissions at this time, work of a better kind, requiring quiet and study. He was willing, and wishing always, to aid his friends, and so for some time he kept up a connection with the paper and made sketches on special occasions.

THE MORNING WALK

His health was delicate, but he was not suffering as in later years ; his spirits were overflowing, and his kindliness and personal charm had made him friends everywhere.

On the 10th of April he enters in his diary— " At Armstrong's all day. Began to paint pigeons on canvas panel. Looking at pigeons in British Museum quadrangle ; " and on the 11th again, "painting pigeons."

On the 15th of April he is " making a drawing of storks, &c.," and on the 17th, 21st, and 22nd, " painting swans at Armstrong's all day."

On the 23rd of April he enters : " Bas-relief hunting scene going on," and on 24th, "painting storks and pigeons," and on 28th, "swans."

The painting of swans, storks, and pigeons, referred to above, was very important work for Caldecott. In conjunction with his friend Mr. Armstrong, he painted the birds in two panels, one of swans (reproduced overleaf), and one of a stork and magpie. These panels were about six feet high, and form part of a series of decorations in the dining-room of Mr. Henry Renshawe's house at Bank Hall, near Buxton, Derbyshire.

The series of decorative paintings (by Thomas Armstrong) which included these panels, was exhibited at Mr. Deschamps' Gallery in New Bond Street in 1874, and attracted much attention at the time. The birds showed to great advantage, and will remain in the memory of many as amongst the most vigorous and effective of Caldecott's paintings in oils. They showed, thus early, a mastery of bird form and a power in reserve of an unusual kind.

"I have paid a little attention to decorative art," he writes to a friend at this time ; besides being "at work on the *Sketch Book*," the results of which will be seen in the next chapter.

Decorative Painting for a Dining-room.

"THE COTTAGE," FARNHAM ROYAL.

CHAPTER VI.

FARNHAM ROYAL, BUCKS.

DURING the summers of 1872, 1873, and 1874, Caldecott stayed often at a cottage belonging to the writer, three miles north of Slough, in Buckinghamshire, in the picturesque neighbourhood of Stoke Pogis and Burnham Beeches.

A "loose box" adjoining the stable—a few yards to the right of the little verandah in the above sketch—had been fitted up for him by friendly hands; and it was here in this temporary studio, in the quiet of the country, looking out on woods and fields, that he made many of the drawings for *Old Christmas.*

Several entries in Caldecott's diary in 1874 mention that in June and July he was "working in the 'loose box' at Farnham Royal, on the *Sketch Book.*"

Those were happy, irresponsible days, before great success had tempered his style, or brought with it many cares. Take the following letter (one of many) written in the full enjoyment of the change from lodgings in London :—

"We are passing a calm and peaceful existence here and were therefore somewhat startled the other day, when Sharp asked for the cart and

donkey to take to the common for the purpose of
bringing us a few Sultanas. We stroked our
beards, but as Sharp seemed bent upon the affair
reluctantly consented."

[The boy Sharp attended to the wants of Caldecott
and his friend L., and wanted to make a pudding.
The end of the letter is reproduced in facsimile.]

THE PADDOCK, FARNHAM ROYAL.

The illustration on the last page is a copy of a water-colour sketch made from "the loose box" at Farnham Royal. It depicts the arrival of a pony at the cottage and consequent disgust of the donkey at the intrusion. The old man—who combined the various offices of gardener, groom, and parish clerk—stood unconsciously as a model for several drawings in *Old Christmas.*

From Farnham Royal he writes at another time to a friend :—

"We are fast drifting into a vortex of dissipation —eddying round a whirlpool of gaiety ; but I hope that through all, our heads will keep clear enough to guide the helms of our hearts."

About this time it was suggested to Caldecott to make studies of animals and birds, with a view to an illustrated edition of *Æsop's Fables*, a work for which his talents seemed eminently fitted. The idea was put aside from press of work, and when finally brought out in 1883 was not the success that had been anticipated. This was principally owing to the plan of the book.

As Caldecott's *Æsop* was often talked over with
the writer in early days, a few words may be
appropriate here.   Caldecott yielded to a sugges-
tion of Mr. J. D. Cooper, the engraver, to attach
to each fable what were to be styled "Modern
Instances," consisting of scenes, social or political,
as an "application."   Humorous as these were, in
the artist's best vein of satire, the combination was

"STUDYING FROM NATURE."

felt to be an artistic mistake.   That Caldecott was
aware of this, almost from the first, is evident from
a few words in a letter to an intimate friend where
he says :—

"Do not expect much from this book. When I see proofs of it I wonder and regret that I did not approach the subject more seriously."

Circumstances of health also in later years interfered with the completion of what might have been his *chef d'œuvre*.

In the following letter to a friend in Manchester (headed with the above sketch) he refers modestly to his drawings for *Old Christmas*, on which he was now busily engaged.

" MY DEAR——,—It is so long since I have heard
from you that I have concluded that you must be
very flourishing in every way. No news being
good news, and no news lasting for so long a time,
you must have a quiver full of good things. How
is—— ? The woods of Dunham ? The gaol of
Knutsford ?—the vale of Knutsford, I mean. A
fortnight ago, when all the
ability were leaving town, I
returned from a six weeks'
pleasant sojourn in Bucks,
at Farnham Royal. I was
hard at work all the time,
for I have been very much
occupied of late, you will
be glad to hear, I know.
In process of time, and
if successful, I will tell
you upon what. I wish I
had had a severe training
for my present profession.
Eating my dinners, so to

ART IS LONG, LIFE IS SHORT.

speak. I have now got a workshop, and I sometimes wish that I was a workman. Art is long :
life isn't. Perhaps you are now careering round
Schleswig or some other-where for a summer
holiday. I shall probably go to France next month
for a business and pleasure excursion. Let me
hear from you about things in general or in par-

ticular—a line, a word will be welcome.   I hope
you are all well ; and with kind regards remain
                    " Yours faithfully,

                            " R. C."

It is clear from the above letter that Caldecott was
conscious of the great change that was coming in his
work in 1874.   The suggestions of his friends that
he should draw continually from familiar objects

" DRAWING FROM FAMILIAR OBJECTS."

and the hints he received from time to time that he
" could not draw a lady," are ludicrously illustrated
in two sketches to a Manchester friend who watched
the progress of the artist with lively interest.

But in spite of his moving laughter, the period
referred to in this chapter was the most serious and

eventful in Caldecott's career ; when a sense of beauty and fitness in design seemed to have been revealed to him, as it were, in a vision, and when his serious studies seemed to be bearing fruit for the first time ; when he felt, as he never felt before, the responsibilities of his art and the

"COULD NOT DRAW A LADY!"

want of severe training for his profession. Then— but not till then—did the lines of *Punch* " On the late Randolph Caldecott," written in February 1886 apply exactly :—

> " Sure never pencil steeped in mirth
> So closely kept to grace and beauty."

* * *

CHAPTER VII.

"OLD CHRISTMAS."

THE "new departure" which Caldecott made in the summer of 1874 will be seen clearly marked in the next few pages, where, with the permission of the publishers, we have reproduced some characteristic drawings from *Old Christmas*.

"There was issued in 1876 by the Messrs. Macmillan" (writes Mr. William Clough, an old and intimate friend of Caldecott) "a book with illustrations that forcibly drew attention to the advent of a new exponent of the pictorial art. These pictures were of so entirely new a nature, and gave such a meaning and emphasis to the text, as to stir even callous bosoms by the graceful and pure creations of the artist's genius. Washington Irving's *Old Christmas* was made alive for us by a new interpreter, who brought grace of drawing with a dainty inventive genius to the delineation of English life in the last century."

It is not generally known that the drawings for *Old Christmas*, one hundred and twelve in number, were all made in 1874; and there is a marked alteration in style during the progress of this book, such as, for example, between the drawing of "The Village Choir" (commenced in March 1874), and the portrait of "Master Simon," placed opposite to each other on pages 96 and 97 of the first edition of *Old Christmas*.

The humour is more robust, but never in after-work was more delightful, than in his rendering of the typical stage coachman. Until these illustrations came it had been said that Washington Irving's coachman stood out as a unique and matchless description of a character that has passed away.

"In the course of a December tour in Yorkshire,"
writes Washington Irving, " I rode for a long
distance on one of the public coaches on the day
preceding Christmas."

Three schoolboys were amongst his fellow-
passengers. " They were under the particular
guardianship of the coachman to whom, whenever
an opportunity presented, they addressed a host of
questions, and pronounced him one of the best
fellows in the world. Indeed I could not but
notice the more than ordinary air of bustle and
importance of the coachman, who wore his hat a
little on one side and had a large bunch of
Christmas green stuck in the button-hole of his coat.

"Wherever an English stage coachman may be
seen he cannot be mistaken for one of any other
craft or mystery. He has commonly a broad full
face, curiously mottled with red, as if the blood had
been forced by hard feeding into every vessel of
the skin; he is swelled into jolly dimensions by
frequent potations of malt liquors, and his bulk
is still further increased by a multiplicity of coats
in which he is buried like a cauliflower, the upper
one reaching to his heels. He wears a broad-
brimmed low-crowned hat; a huge roll of coloured
handkerchief about his neck, knowingly knotted and
tucked in at the bosom, and has in summer-time a
large bouquet of flowers in his button-hole, the
present most probably of some enamoured country

lass. His waistcoat is commonly of some bright colour, striped ; and his small clothes extend far below the knees to meet a pair of jockey-boots which reach about halfway up his legs.

THE STAGE COACHMAN.

" All this costume is maintained with much precision ; he has a pride in having his clothes of excellent materials ; and notwithstanding the seeming grossness of his appearance, there is still discernible that neatness and propriety of person which is almost inherent in an Englishman. He

enjoys great consequence and consideration along
the road; has frequent conferences with the village
housewives, who look upon him as a man of great

IN THE STABLE YARD.

trust and dependence; and he seems to have a
good understanding with every bright-eyed lass.
The moment he arrives he throws down the reins
with something of an air, and abandons the cattle to

the care of the ostler; his duty being merely to drive from one stage to another. When off the box his hands are thrust in the pockets of his greatcoat, and he rolls about the inn yard with an air of the most absolute lordliness. Here he is generally surrounded by an admiring throng of ostlers, stable-boys, shoe-blacks, and those nameless hangers-on that infest inns and taverns and run errands. Every ragamuffin that has a coat to his back thrusts his hands in his pockets, rolls in his gait, talks slang, and is an embryo 'coachey.'"

Surely it has seldom happened in the history of illustration that an author should be so very closely followed—if not overtaken—by his illustrator. No literary touch seemed to be wanting from the author to convey a picture of English life and character passed away; but Caldecott's coachman helps to elucidate the text; and whilst it carried to many a reader of *Old Christmas* in the New World a living portrait of a past age, it revealed also the presence of a new illustrator.

Here was a reproachful lesson. The art of illustration—an art untaught in England and unconsidered by too many—was shown in all its strength and usefulness by a comparatively new hand.

Of the numerous illustrations drawn by Caldecott in 1874 for *Old Christmas*, we may select as examples the young Oxonian leading out one of his maiden aunts at a dance on Christmas Eve ; and " the fair Julia" in the intervals of dancing listening with apparent indifference to a song from her admirer ; amusing herself the while by plucking to pieces a choice bouquet of hothouse flowers.

THE TROUBADOUR..

The style and treatment of the drawing, on the opposite page, differs from anything previously done by Caldecott, and would hardly have been recognised as his work ; the handling is less firm, and colour and quality have been more considered in deference

The Fair Julia.

to what was considered the public taste in such
matters. But in a few pages he emancipates himself again, and gives us some brilliant character
sketches. In the last example from *Old Christmas*
he is in his element. Nothing could be more
characteristic, or in touch with the period illustrated,
than the picture of Frank Bracebridge, Master
Simon, and the author of *Old Christmas*, walking
about the grounds of the family mansion "escorted
by a number of gentleman-like dogs, from the
frisking spaniel to the steady old staghound.
The dogs were all obedient to a dog-whistle which
hung to Master Simon's button-hole, and in the
midst of the gambols would glance an eye oc-
casionally upon a small switch he carried in his
hand."[1] Thus the minute observation of the writer
is closely followed by the illustrator, who here from
his own habit of close observation of the ways
of animals, was enabled to give additional completeness to the picture ; and the effect was greatly
heightened by a wise determination on the part

---

[1] It was more than once suggested to Caldecott to paint this scene. It
would probably have been attempted had circumstances permitted.

of Mr. Cooper the engraver, that the illustrations should be " so mingled with the text that both united should form one picture." This book was engraved at leisure, and not published until the end of 1875, by Messrs. Macmillan & Co., bearing date 1876.

It is interesting to note that *Old Christmas* was offered to, and declined by, one of the leading publishers in London ; principally on the

MASTER SIMON AND HIS DOGS.

ground that the illustrations were considered " in-
artistic, flippant and vulgar, and unworthy of the
author of *Old Christmas* " !   It was not until 1876
that the world discovered a new genius.

During the progress of the drawings for *Old
Christmas* in 1874, Caldecott went with the writer
to Brittany to make sketches for a new book ;
but the publication was postponed until after a
more extended tour in 1878.

These summer wanderings of Caldecott in
Brittany were prolific of work ; his pencil and note-
book were never at rest, as the pages of *Breton
Folk* testify (see Chapter xi.).   The drawings,
both in 1874 and in 1878, mark a strong artistic
advance upon similar work in the Harz Mountains.   His feeling for the sentiment and beauty
of landscape, especially the open land,—generally
absent from the sketches in the Harz Mountains,
—is noticeable here.   The statuesque grace of
the younger women, the picturesqueness of costume, operations of husbandry, outdoor *fêtes*
and the like, and the open air effect of nearly
every group of figures seen in these summer

journeys—all came as delightful material for his pencil.

Caldecott's studies with M. Dalou, the sculptor,

ON THE ROAD SIDE, BRITTANY.

in 1874, and the great proficiency he had already obtained in modelling in clay, enabled him to make several successful groups from his Brittany subjects.

The bright-eyed stolid child in sabots at the roadside (one of the first of the quaint little figures that attracted his attention in Brittany) stands on

the writer's table in concrete presentment in clay;
the model is not much larger than the sketch—
the front, the profile, and the back view, each
forming a separate and faithful study from life.

The young mother and child in the cathedral
at Guingamp (reproduced opposite) was another
successful effort in modelling, but Caldecott was not
satisfied with it excepting as a rough sketch—
" a recollection in clay."

It is interesting here to note the handling of
the artist in his favourite material, French clay.
The model stands but six inches high, but it was
intended to have reproduced it larger. Another
sketch in the round was of "a pig of Brittany,"
reproduced on page 194.

"Save up," he writes about this time to a
friend in Manchester, "and be an art patron; you
will soon be able to buy some interesting terra
cottas by R. C.!"

This was a heavy year, for many illustrations
were produced not mentioned in these pages; and
in October he was busy on the wax bas-relief of
a " Brittany horse fair," afterwards cast in metal

AT GUINGAMP, BRITTANY.
Facsimile of Model in Terra Cotta, 1874.

and exhibited in the Royal Academy in 1876 (see page 137).

On the 19th of November and following days

To M. H.—Christmas, 1874.

Caldecott was "working at Dalou's on a cat crouching for a spring." He had a skeleton of a cat, a dead cat, and a live cat to work from. This model in clay was finished on the 8th December, 1874.

Christmas Eve was spent " in the caverns of the British Museum making a drawing, and measuring skeleton of a white stork." This was a most elaborate and careful record of measurements. On the 28th of December he was "engaged on brown paper cartoon of storks at Armstrong's," and on the 30th is the entry,—"at British Museum; had storks out of cases to examine insertion of wing feathers."

Thus, all through the year 1874 Caldecott, working without much recognition excepting from a few intimates, got through an immense amount of work; not forgetting his friends the children, to whom he sent many Christmas greetings with letters and coloured sketches. The drawing on the opposite page accompanied a kindly letter to a child of six years.

" I thank you," he says, " very much for your grand sheet of drawings, which I think are very nice indeed. I hope you will go on trying and learning to draw. There are many beautiful things waiting to be drawn. Animals and flowers oh ! such a many—and a few people."

The last sketch in 1874—a postscript to a private
letter—tells its own story.

CHAPTER VIII.

LETTERS, DIAGRAMS, ETC.

In a letter to a friend in Manchester, on the 17th January, 1875, Caldecott writes :—

"I stick pretty close to business, pretty much in that admirable and attentive manner which was the delight, the pride, the exultation of the great chiefs who strode it through the Manchester banking halls. Yes, I have not forsaken those gay—though perhaps, to the heart yearning to be fetterless, irksome—scenes without finding that the world ever requires toil from those sons of labour who would be successful.

"However, during the last year I managed to do a lot of work away from town, and enjoyed it. Sometimes it was expensive, because when at the cottage in Bucks, we of course mixed with the county families and had to 'keep a carriage' to return calls, return from dinner, and so forth."

AT FARNHAM ROYAL—RETURNING VISITS.

Here is "a meditation for the New Year"—

"You will excuse me," he says, "talking of myself when I tell you that amongst the resolutions for the New Year was one only to talk of matters about which there was a reasonable probability that I knew something. Now human beings are a mystery to me, and taking them all round I think we may consider them a failure. If I do not understand anything that belongs to myself, how can I understand what belongeth to another? This, my dear W., with your clear · intellect, you will see is sound.

"I often think of the scenes and faces and jokes of banking days, and have amongst them many pleasant reminiscences. Perhaps we shall all meet again in that land which lies round the corner!"

[Here follows a grotesque sketch of a man on a winter's day, with an umbrella, hurrying off to the "Nag and Nosebag."]

SUNRISE.

At the beginning of 1875, in the intervals of book illustration, Caldecott was busy "working on a cartoon of storks." This was a design for a picture in oils, painted in March and afterwards bought by Mr. F. Pennington, late M.P. for Stockport.

On the 7th of January he enters in his diary, "Painted some storks on the wing for a panel for a

wardrobe." The rendering of dawn on the upmost clouds, the storks rising from the dark earth to greet the sun, can hardly be indicated without colour, but the design is given accurately. It was a poetic fancy which he had had in his

STUDY IN LINE.   mind for some time; one of many half developed designs which, if his health had permitted, the world might have seen more of.

On the 25th of January he "made a dry point sketch of a Quimperlé Brittany woman," and in February he was busy modelling as usual.

On the 5th of February, "took to Lucchesi (moulder) wax bas-relief of horse fair, and small 'sketch' of brewers' waggon."

The advance of the art of reproducing drawings in facsimile in a cheap form, suitable for printing at the type press like wood engravings, was attracting much attention in England in 1875, and at the writer's request Caldecott made a series of diagrams sugges-

STUDY IN LINE.

YOUTH & AGE

DIAGRAM.   DESIGN FOR A PICTURE, 1875.

tive of the power of line and of effects to be
obtained by simple methods, to illustrate a paper
read before the Society of Arts in London in
March, 1875, on "The Art of Illustration."

With his usual kindness and enthusiasm he put
aside his work—some modelling in clay which he
had been studying under his friend M. Dalou, the
French sculptor—and at once began a diagram,
about seven feet by five feet, to suggest a picture in

A MAD DOG.

DIAGRAM.

the simplest way. Without much consideration, without models, and in the limited area of his little studio in Great Russell Street, Bloomsbury, he set to work with a brush on the broad white sheet, and in about an hour produced the drawing in line of " Youth and Age " on the last page.

The horses were not quite satisfactory to himself; but the sentiment of the picture, the open

air effect of early spring, the crisp grass, the birds'
nests forming in the almost leafless trees, the
effect of distance indicated in a few lines—and
above all, the feeling of sky produced by the *un-*

DIAGRAM.   "THE LECTURER."

touched background—were skilfully suggested in the
large diagram.

On other occasions, and for the same lecture, he
made several other diagrams, including one of the

DIAGRAM.

pursuit of a dog in a village, another of a lecturer and various heads in an audience. The reproductions are interesting to examine together as early work in a style in which he afterwards was famous —a style, which was *not outline* in the strict sense of the word, and which to a great extent was his own. It had little in common with Flaxman, it was not in the manner of Gillray, Cruikshank, Doyle, or Leech ; nor in the more academic manner of his friend—and predecessor in children's books—Walter Crane.

To these somewhat tentative drawings he afterwards added to the series a diagram, six feet high, of the famous mad dog from one of his Picture Books, and another of the figure of a child running, reproduced above.

The discovery of a process by which a drawing

on paper in line, could be photographed and brought into relief, like a wood-block for printing at the type press, was not perfected in England until 1875, and did not come into general use until 1876 ; had it come a year or two earlier it would have had an important influence upon Caldecott's work.

DIAGRAM.

Without going too far into technicalities, it may be interesting to illustrators to mention here that all Caldecott's best drawings in his Picture Books, *John Gilpin*, *The House that Jack Built*, &c. ; in the *Graphic* newspaper, and in Washington Irving's

Old Christmas, &c., were photographed on to wood-blocks and have passed through the hands of the engraver.

The system of photographic engraving (by which the drawings are reproduced on pp. 124 and 125) bids fair to supersede wood-engraving for rapid journalistic purposes. It naturally attracted Caldecott in the first instance ; but with increased knowledge and perception of "values," and of the quality to be obtained in a good wood-engraving above any mechanical reproduction in relief, Caldecott was glad to avail himself of the help of the engraver. He drew with greater freedom, as he expressed it, preferring, as so many illustrators do, to put in tints with a brush, to be rendered in line by skilful engravers. But at the same time he delighted in shewing the *power of line* in drawing, studying "the art of leaving out as a science" ; doing nothing hastily but thinking long and seriously before putting pen to paper, remembering, as he always said, "the fewer the lines, the less error committed."

In the spring of 1875 he sends this lively picture.

of himself from Dodington, near Whitchurch, in
Shropshire, where he had been working, staying
with friends, in the full enjoyment of country life.

Writing on the 27th of April, 1875, he says :—

"I feel I owe somebody an apology for staying
in the country so long, but don't quite see to whom
it is due, so I shall stay two or three days longer,
and then I shall indeed hang my harp on a willow

tree. It is difficult to screw up the proper amount of courage for leaving the lambkins, the piglets, the foals, the goslings, the calves, and the puppies. We want rain, and then things will grow with exceeding speed; as it is, the earth is dry and the buds are slow to display their hidden beauties. A little of 'something to drink' will cheer them, and then, like some human beings, they will look pleasant and cheerful and 'come out.'"

Next, from a letter to an intimate friend, dated 5th March, 1875, on being asked to become a trustee :—

"The event is of a pleasing nature because it shows that somebody still believes in the continuance of that uprightness of principle, rectitude of conduct, and general respectability of mind and heart which for so many years endeared me to the nobility, clergy, gentry, gasmen, and fowl stealers of W———."

Life in the country with Caldecott was "worth living," and he chafed much at this period if he had to be with his "nose to the grindstone," as he expressed it, in Bloomsbury. Whilst in the country

his letters to town were full of sketches, but in letters
from London he hardly ever pictured life out of
doors.

"SHOWS HIS TERRA COTTAS."

In June 1875, he shows the bas-relief of "A
Boar Hunt," and some small groups in terra cotta,
to his friends.[1]

Before the favourable verdict of the press was
pronounced on *Old Christmas*, Caldecott was com-
missioned to illustrate a second volume ; and, in
May 1875, he was already at work making studies
and drawings for *Bracebridge Hall*, which did not
appear until the end of 1876.

---

[1] The medallion at the head of this letter was designed by Sir Frederick
Burton and afterwards redrawn for the Arts Club by E. J. Poynter, R.A.

About this time the first number of *Academy
Notes* was published, and in a postscript to a letter
to the writer (of too private a nature to be printed)
Caldecott pictures its "first appearance in a family
circle."

THE FIRST YEAR OF ACADEMY NOTES.

In June 1875, Caldecott had "three drawings
in sepia, badly hung, in the 'black and white'
exhibition at the Dudley Gallery."

On the 4th of August he was "making designs
for pelican picture;" and afterwards studying this
subject at the Zoological Gardens. Two pictures
of pelicans were eventually painted; the second,

in the possession of Mr. W. Phipson Beale, is
sketched below.

THREE PELICANS AND TORTOISE (OIL PAINTING).

Writing on the 10th August, 1875, respecting
some Cretan embroideries just arrived in England,
he sends the sketch overleaf.

"In accordance with your letter about the embroideries," he says, " I have placed the address of the
importer in the hands of Mr. N., a man well-skilled
in detecting that which is good in a crowd of works

of art.   He is great in pottery, embroidery and

INSPECTING EMBROIDERIES.

decoration ; but he has a mind great in forgetting,
and a fine talent for losing addresses."

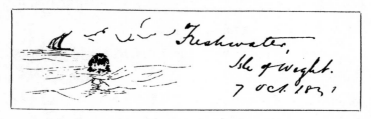

In October, whilst at the seaside, he " made six

drawings;" and, later in the year, was "modelling panels for Lord Monteagle's chimney-piece."

In November 1875 he received the first copy of *Old Christmas* from the publishers, and already favourable notices of the illustrations had begun to appear in the newspapers.

A CHRISTMAS CARD TO K. E. B.

READING "OPINIONS OF THE PRESS" ON "OLD CHRISTMAS."

CHAPTER IX.

ROYAL ACADEMY, "BRACEBRIDGE HALL," ETC.

THE "opinions of the press" on Washington Irving's *Old Christmas*, which Mr. J. D. Cooper, the wood engraver, is depicted reading to the artist with so much glee, were all that could be desired ; and they fully justified the second venture (*Bracebridge Hall*), on which Caldecott was already engaged.

In February he was "painting a frieze for Mr. Pennington's drawing room" at Broome Hall, Holmwood, Sussex ; and, later on, was "carving panels for a chimneypiece."

In this year, 1876, Caldecott exhibited his first painting in the Royal Academy, entitled, "There were Three Ravens sat on a Tree." The humour and vigour of the composition are well indicated in the sketch. It was hung rather out of sight, above (and in somewhat grim proximity with) a picture of "At Death's Door," by Hubert Herkomer. Both artists were then thirty years of age.

Cat. No 415.   49 × 32.

"THERE WERE THREE RAVENS SAT ON A TREE."

(Oil Painting) Royal Academy, 1876.

In the same room (Gallery V.) were collected that year, the works of painters whose names are familiar —W. B. Richmond, A. Gow, H. R. Robertson,

E. H. Fahey, W. W. Ouless, Val C. Prinsep, Henry Moore, and others.

Besides "The Three Ravens" he exhibited in 1876 the metal bas-relief of a "Horse Fair in Brittany," reproduced opposite. This was a more masterful production than the picture, and attracted

"Private view of my first R.A. picture," April 1876.

great attention in the Royal Academy Exhibition. It was mentioned in the *Times* of that year, and in the *Saturday Review*, June 10th, 1876, we read :—

"Of low relief—taking the Elgin frieze as the standard—one of the purest examples we have seen for many a day is Mr. Caldecott's bas-relief, "A Horse Fair in Brittany." Here a simple and almost rude incident in nature has been brought within the laws and symmetry of art."

Cat. No. 1499.

"A Horse Fair in Brittany."

Metal bas-relief exhibited in the Royal Academy, 1876.

Size 14 × 5½ in.

In 1876 Caldecott also produced a relief in metal of " A Boar Hunt," which was exhibited in the Grosvenor Gallery in 1878.

To the world at large and in the opinion of many critics, there was, in his Academy work of 1876, promise of an exceptionally successful career. Decorative design and modelling in relief were Caldecott's especial forte, and it is to be regretted that so few of these works remain to us. " The Horse Fair in Brittany," in the possession of the writer, is one of the few completed works of this character. He was not destined to be a prolific painter, although strongly urged at this time by members of the Royal Academy to devote his energies to painting. Neither his health nor his previous training justified his leaving a branch of art in which he was already becoming famous, that of book illustration.

In 1876 the system of reproducing sketches in pen and ink by photo-engraving became general in England, and in the pages of *Academy Notes* of that year there appeared, for the first time, sketches by the painters of their exhibited works.

Amongst well-known artists — who powerfully aided in founding a system of illustration which was destined to spread over the world—were Sir John Gilbert, R.A., H. Stacy Marks, R.A., Marcus Stone, A.R.A., and, the comparatively young, Randolph Caldecott. The three first-named are masters in line each in his own style, and their methods were studied and imitated by many other painters in England to whom line drawing was then a sealed book. Several sketches of pictures in the *Academy Notes*, 1876, were drawn by Caldecott, including the portrait of Captain Burton, painted by Sir Frederick Leighton, P. R. A.

CAPTAIN BURTON, R.A., 1876.

In June he made a series of illustrations, entitled "Christmas Visitors," for the *Graphic* newspaper ; and about this time the drawings for *Bracebridge Hall* were finished.

BRACEBRIDGE HALL.

" THE success of *Old Christmas* has suggested the re-publication of its sequel, *Bracebridge Hall*, illustrated by the same able pencil, but condensed, so as to bring it within reasonable size and price."

FACSIMILE OF FIRST PAGE OF "BRACEBRIDGE HALL."

"THE CHIVALRY OF THE HALL PREPARED TO TAKE THE FIELD."

In *Bracebridge Hall* we meet the fair Julia again in one of the most graceful illustrations Caldecott ever drew. An extract from the text is necessary to show the subtle touch of the illustrator.

" I have derived much pleasure," says Washington Irving, "from observing the fair Julia and her lover . . . I observed them yesterday in the garden advancing along one of the retired walks. The sun was shining with delicious warmth, making great masses of bright verdure and deep blue shade. The cuckoo, that harbinger of spring, was faintly heard from a distance; the thrush piped from the hawthorn, and the yellow butterflies sported, and toyed and coquetted in the air.

" The fair Julia was leaning on her lover's arm, listening to his conversation with her eyes cast down, a soft blush on her cheek and a quiet smile on her lips, while in the hand which hung negligently by her side was a bunch of flowers. In this way they were sauntering slowly along, and when I considered them, and the scenery in which they were moving, I could not but think it a thousand pities that the season should ever change or that young people should ever grow older, or that blossoms should give way to fruit or that lovers should ever get married." The harmony here between author and illustrator needs no comment.

THE FAIR JULIA AND HER LOVER.

There were 120 drawings made for *Bracebridge Hall*, remarkable for artistic qualities and fully sustaining the reputation of the artist.

The originals were drawn about one third larger, in pen and ink, photographed on wood and engraved

"GENERAL HARBOTTLE AT DINNER."

in facsimile. The effect of many of the drawings in the first editions was injured by the want of margin on the printed page; but an *édition de luxe* is now printed with *Old Christmas* and *Bracebridge Hall* in one volume.

As it is the object of this memoir to record facts —and as the originator of good ideas is seldom recognised—it should be stated here that it is owing to Mr. Cooper, the engraver, that Washington Irving's books were ever illustrated by Caldecott. The idea, he says in the preface, "has been delayed in execution for many years, mainly from the difficulty of finding an artist capable of identifying himself with the author;" modestly adding —"whether this result has now been attained or no, must be left to the verdict of the lovers of the gifted writer in both hemispheres."

"An Extinguisher."

The two next sketches mark with touching emphasis the serious change in Caldecott's health which
took place in the autumn of this year.

In August he is writing from the country in high
spirits as usual, and planning out much work for the
future. *Bracebridge Hall* was finished, and the
success of *Old Christmas* had brought him many
commissions.   His illustrations on wood had turned
out well, being fortunate in his engravers, especially
Mr. J. D. Cooper and Mr. Edmund Evans, who
always rendered his work with sympathetic care.
He may also be said to have been fortunate in
his connection with the *Graphic* newspaper under
the direction of Mr. W. L. Thomas, the artist and
wood engraver.

But alas! in the autumn of this year his health
failed him, and in October he was advised to go
to Buxton in Derbyshire.

On the 2nd November, 1876, he writes :—

AT BUXTON.

" I am as above.   Walking solemnly in the
gardens, or sitting limply in the almost deserted
saloon listening to an enfeebled band."

The result of that visit was a series of delightful
sketches, which appeared in the *Graphic* newspaper,
the originals of which are in the possession of
Mr. Samuel Pope, Q.C.

A CHRISTMAS CARD.

CHAPTER X.

ON THE RIVIERA.

THE journey to the Riviera and North Italy, which Caldecott was compelled to make for his health, before Christmas 1876, was as usual prolific of work. Writing from Monaco in January, 1877, he says :—

"This is a beautiful place, and for the benefit of you stay-at-home bodies I will describe it—in my way ;" and in four original letters published in the *Graphic* newspaper in March and April, 1877, there appeared about sixty illustrations containing upwards of three hundred figures, different studies of life and character; and these drawings do not represent probably, one half of the sketches made.

No such pictures of Monte Carlo and its neighbourhood had been sent home before; they were the ideal newspaper correspondent's letters—the sketches abounding in humour and accurate detail; the letters accompanying them being written from personal observation.

It would have been strange indeed if these letters had not attracted general attention and amusement in a newspaper; but they did more than this, they revealed an amount of artistic insight, and suggested possibilities in Caldecott's future career as an artist which his health never permitted him to put to the test.

At Monaco and at Monte Carlo, Caldecott found so much that suited his pencil that it is a wonder that he found time for any more serious work. With touches of satire that remind us of Thackeray, and a gaiety all his own, these spontaneous and delightful letters form the best picture of Caldecott that can be given in 1877.

"Round the tables," he writes, "from noon to nearly midnight—seven days a week—the *monde élégant* congregates, from the Yorkshireman to the Japanese." Then follow sketches of an Englishman in Scotch tweed, and a young man from Japan. Next is a general sketch of the crowd at the round table, the artist's own figure, admirably given, standing back to us, hat in hand. It was a marvellous gathering presented on the printed page, "all intent on gambling—editors of journals, English justices of the peace, venerable matrons and innocent girls, beloved sons who are 'travelling,' artistes, chevaliers of the legion of honour, dames who are not of that legion." "Such costumes and toilettes sweep the polished floor, such delicately-gloved fingers clutch the glittering coins—when they happen to win, and sometimes when they don't—such a clinking of money, as the croupiers mass the rakings."

From the fashionable crowd and the heated atmosphere of the Casino the artist takes us along the cool shores of the Mediterranean, where, in one of the best sketches in these letters, full of air and

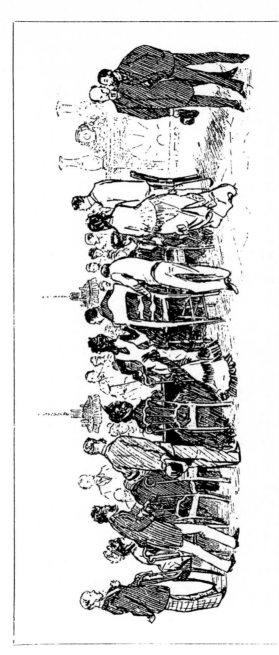

The Gaming Tables at Monte Carlo.

light, he brings two figures into unexpected contrast. "Walking one afternoon along the Mentone road, we reached a point commanding a fine view of sea, hills, and olive trees. There was a stone seat, and on it an aged round-backed man. On the wall and bench before him were spread out many cards dotted with the results of numerous twirls of the roulette ball. He was studying his chances for the future. As we turned away we met a priest reading in a little book as he passed."

As the landscapes suffered in reproduction in the newspaper, and were the least successful part in these letters, it may be well to mention that some of Caldecott's landscape studies in oils and water colours, on the shores of the Mediterranean, were the best he ever did, attracting much attention at the sale of his works in 1886.

That he did not put a high estimate on his powers as a landscape painter at that time may be gathered from a few words in a private letter declining some commissions.

"The drawings that G. so kindly enquires about are not in my line. I would rather not attempt to

"Priest and Player."

paint what I imagine he wants—proper professional water-colour landscape painter's work.

" Please say that my line is to make to smile the lunatic who has shown no sign of mirth for many months (see the *Graphic* of Saturday last, 6th January, p. 7, right-hand column—I tumbled upon it in the reading room of the Casino), and not to portray the beauties of this southern clime— not but what I would if I could ! "

NORTH ITALIAN FOLK.

It was in the same winter, during his journey in North Italy, that Caldecott made twenty-eight illustrations for a book on *North Italian Folk.*[1] Here Caldecott's studies, and his habit of sketching the peasantry wherever he went, served him well.

Take the picture of the priest and his faithful servant Caterina ; the latter, reproaching her master for bringing home a neighbour, Maddalena, " to eat two *lasagne* with us ! " Caterina is "a gaunt threadbare-looking woman of some five-and-thirty

---

[1] *North Italian Folk*, by Mrs. Comyns Carr. London : Chatto and Windus, 1878.

years, and the *prevosto* is gaunt too, and sallow;
the two match well together. Caterina's hair is
smooth though scant, and her faded print dress is

THE PRIEST'S SERVANT ADMINISTERS A REPROOF.

neat, but the bright yellow kerchief round her
shoulders is soiled, and the cunning plaits of her
grey hair are not as well ordered as the women's
are wont to be on mass days.

"Presently Caterina bustles into the darkened
parlour, where sits the *prevosto* lazily smoking his

pipe and reading the country newspaper. He has
put aside even the least of his clerical garments
now, and lounges at ease in an old coat and slippers,
his tonsured head covered by a battered straw hat.

" ' Listen to me,' breaks forth the faithful woman,
and she is not careful to modulate her voice even
to a semblance of secrecy, ' you don't bring another
mouth for me to feed here when it is baking day
again. *Per Bacco*, no indeed ! . . It sha'n't happen
again, do you hear ? And I have the holy wafers to
bake besides. For shame of you ! Come now to
your dinner in the kitchen !' And Caterina, the better
for this free expression, hastens to dish up the
minestra.

" ' Poor old priest ! What a shrew he has got in
in his house,' says some pitying reader. Yet he
would not part with her for worlds ! She is his solace
and his right hand, and loves him none the less
because of her sharp tongue and uncurbed speech.
In many a lone and cheerless home of Italian priest
can I call to mind such a woman as this—such a
fond and faithful drudge, with harsh ways and a
soft heart."

Another picture in *North Italian Folk* seems to
give the character of the peasantry and the scenery
exactly. " The sun glitters on the pale sea that is

down and away a mile or more beyond the sloping
fields and gardens, and the dipping valley. Giovanni

THE HUSBANDMAN.

pauses to rest his burthen upon the wall just where
the way turns to the right again, leaving the mountains and chestnut-clad hills behind it."

GOSSIP.

Here in the sketch we are made to feel the sunlight and the glare from the sea on the southern slope; every detail of the pathway, to the stones in the old wall, being accurately given.

Never, perhaps, in any book since Washington Irving's *Old Christmas* and *Bracebridge Hall* was the illustrator more in touch with the author than in *North Italian Folk;* but for some reason —probably because Caldecott's work and style had become identified with English people and their ways, both abroad and at home—the illustrations made little impression. The completeness of the pictures, and the local colour infused into them by the author, left little to be done; moreover, Caldecott was not on his own ground, and to draw buildings and landscape in black and white, with the finish, and what is technically called the "colour," considered necessary for a book of this kind, was always irksome to him.

Less characteristic, but charming as a drawing, is the group of country girls under the cherry trees, reproduced on the opposite page. It is a picture worth having for its own sake, whether it aid the

"DIGNITY AND IMPUDENCE."

text or not, and one with which we may fitly leave this volume.

Early in the year 1877 Caldecott made several drawings for an illustrated catalogue of the National Gallery. Amongst the best in the English section were the two sketches from Sir Edwin Landseer's pictures, reproduced here. The grave portrait of an old bloodhound in " Dignity and Impudence," and the animation and movement in the diminutive poodle by his side,

" SPANIELS, KING CHARLES'S BREED."   SIR E. LANDSEER, R.A.

are indicated in a few expressive lines. The
bright eyes of the two little spaniels of King

PORTRAIT OF A LAWYER BY MORONI.

Charles's breed glitter under his hand in the
original pen and ink sketch.

For the foreign section of the book on the

National Gallery he made many sketches, notably one of the " Portrait of a Lawyer " by Moroni. Here the touch and method of line are different; quality was more considered, and an attempt made to give something of the effect of the picture.

But neither he, nor those with whom he worked in those days, had mastered the best methods of drawing for mechanical reproduction, as they are understood now; fascinating as it seemed to him, and to many other illustrators also, to learn that the time had come when, by mechanical— or more properly chemical—engraving, the touch of the pen could be printed on the page.

It may be said generally in 1877, that Caldecott disliked drawing for " process," and that after years of experience, and having achieved most successful results by photographic engraving, he remained faithful to the wood engraver. The delicate little drawings in brown ink, which were dispersed in hundreds under the auctioneer's hammer in June, 1886, had nearly all been photographed on to wood blocks.

In June, 1877, Caldecott—staying at Shaldon,

Teignmouth, South Devon, for the benefit of his health, chafing under enforced idleness and "debarred by the doctors from all sport," as he says—writes a letter with the following little sketch of "Waiting for a Boat."

"WAITING FOR A BOAT."

"The weather has been unwell for many of the days, and has much interfered with the intellectual occupation of enticing 'dabs' on to hooks let down into the sea by pieces of string and concealed by shreds of mussels.

"On only one occasion have I been engaged in this exciting pursuit—all chases and pursuits are more or less exciting—but this one on that account can hardly be considered 'detrimental' to

my health.   There were three of us in the boat
when I engaged in the sport.   We had a large can
of fine mussels.   We threw out the lines and hauled
them in every now and then, for three good hours,
being about a mile out to sea.   Two whole dabs
were the result.   I was quite calm as we rowed
home.

"I do not boast of this exploit, although the
larger dab was at least seven inches long by four
and a half wide, and fully $\frac{3}{8}$ of an inch thick.   Still
I glow a little as I recount his measurements."

Many illustrations were made in the autumn of
1877 for the *Graphic* and other publications which
need not be detailed.   A painting of one of his
favourite hunting scenes was also in progress, in
spite of dark days and delicate health.

"CLEOPATRA."

CHAPTER XI.

"BRETON FOLK," ETC.

For Mr. Frederick Locker-Lampson, the poet, Caldecott made in the years 1877-8, twelve drawings to illustrate *Bramble Rise, A Winter Phantasy, My Neighbour Rose*, and other verses. These illustrations, most delicately drawn in pen and ink, have not yet been published. One was used in 1881 in a privately printed edition of the *London Lyrics*, and three in 1883, in a little volume of the *Lyrics*

printed by the "Book Fellows Club" in New
York. Caldecott afterwards made four illustrations
for Mrs. Locker-Lampson's child's book, *What the
Blackbird Said*, and two years afterwards, in 1882,
an illustration to her *Greystoke Hall.* These two
books are published by Messrs. Routledge.

In 1878 he exhibited his picture of "The
Three Huntsmen" riding home in evening light.
It was hung rather high in Gallery VII. at the
Royal Academy Exhibition, and technically could
hardly be pronounced a success; but it was a distinct
advance on previous exhibited work, and drew
the serious attention of critics to Caldecott as a
painter. The sketch appeared in an article on
the Academy in *L'Art*, vol. xx. p. 211. Of
this oil painting, Mr. Mundella, the late President
of the Board of Trade writes :—

"The picture was bought by me of poor Caldecott in 1878.
I think it was exhibited at the Royal Academy in that year, but I
bought it from his easel. It is an oil painting, 3 ft. 6 in. by
2 ft. 9 in., and the subject is the 'Three Huntsmen.' I remember
his bringing the song to my house after the purchase, and reading
the song with great enjoyment, pointing out to us how he had
illustrated the verse, 'We hunted and we holloed till the setting
of the sun.' My little granddaughter (Millais' 'Dorothy Thorpe')
was his model for several of his Christmas books. She is the

THE THREE HUNTSMEN (OIL PAINTING).
Royal Academy, 1878.

little girl in *Sing a Song of Sixpence* and several others, and possesses copies sent by him with little sketches and dedications. He is indeed a national loss."

In the Grosvenor Gallery of the same year Caldecott exhibited a small metal bas-relief of " A Boar Hunt," of which he made the following sketch in *Grosvenor Notes.*

No. 232.   8 in. × 18 in.
" A BOAR HUNT " (BAS-RELIEF).   Grosvenor Gallery, 1878.

Special interest attaches to this design, also to " The Horse Fair in Brittany," reproduced on page 137, for the insight it gives of Caldecott's varied artistic powers, which, by force of circumstances, were always held in reserve. If, as a writer remarks, " The treatment of reliefs is a test of the state of a school of sculpture," these examples may help to "place" Caldecott amongst contemporary artists.

Early in 1878, Mr. Edmund Evans, the wood engraver, came to him with a proposal that he should illustrate some books for children to be printed in colours. The plan was soon decided upon, and the first of the *Picture Books* was begun. In the summer of the same year, Caldecott went with the writer for a second time to Brittany.

It was at first intended to take a gig and drive through and through, the country, giving an account of adventures from day to day, and Caldecott (who was more at home perhaps, in a gig than in any other position of life) favoured the idea; but time and other circumstances prevented.

The next proposal was to give a general description of the country and its people, its churches and ruined castles, as they exist to-day. But Caldecott did not take to this idea; he never in his lifetime drew buildings with the same facility as figures, and, at that time, to attempt to make drawings of chateaux, cathedrals and the like, would have been unsuccessful. So the book,

Brittany Picturesque, which had already been partly written, was laid aside to give space for sketches of *Breton Folk.*[1]

" THE TRAP."

"We obtained a trap in a few days"—not the gig, independent of a driver, which Caldecott always sighed for. His delight and high spirits on the first journey, in 1874, are seen in the sketch where he is waving farewell to some astonished peasantry. To be "on the road" was always a pleasure to Caldecott, from the "old Whitchurch days," which

---

[1] *Breton Folk,* by Henry Blackburn, with 170 illustrations by R. Caldecott. London : Sampson Low and Co., 1880.

he often described to his friends—driving home in
the dark at reckless speed after a late supper, in a
dog-cart full of rather uproarious company—down
to 1885 at Frensham, when as host, he would drive
his friends in the lanes of Surrey.

At least 200 sketches must have been made in

SKETCHING UNDER DIFFICULTIES.

these journeys; besides jottings of heads, figures
and the like, and several drawings in water colours.

The summer fêtes and "pardons," all through the

country, furnished capital material for his pencil, the
women's caps of different districts were each recorded,
and here and there a solemn suggestive landscape
noted for a picture which was never to be completed.

BRETON FARMER AND CATTLE.

The circumstances under which some of the
sketches were made is indicated on page 171.

One of the first drawings made in Brittany, both
in colour and black and white (a scene of which
Caldecott was always desirous of making a finished
picture), was the buckwheat harvest, with the
women at work in the fields. Many similar scenes
were put down in note-books, many were the studies

of clouds careering over the wind-blown land,
which were never engraved or published.

Two of the principal events in these journeys
were visits to a horse fair at Le Folgoet, and to a

A WAYSIDE CROSS.

cattle fair at Carhaix, where Caldecott made the
following sketches :—

"Le Folgoet is in the north of Finisterre, in the
north-west corner of Brittany. The country is for

the most part flat and dreary in aspect; a few fields
of buckwheat, corn, and rye are passed on the road,
protected by banked-up hedges, and skirted by
pollard trees.

AT THE HORSE FAIR, LE FOLGOET.

"On the road as we approach the fair, a mile and
a half from the town, is a characteristic figure, a
barefooted *gamin* with red cap and grey jersey
trotting out an old chestnut mare." As he stops

and turns to look back, he is thus rapidly recorded in a sketch.

Apart from the artistic material so abundant everywhere, Caldecott's love for animals and knowledge of them, his interest in everything connected

TROTTING OUT HORSES AT CARHAIX.

with farming, markets, country life and surroundings, roused him to exertions at Carhaix which none but the most hardy "special artist" would have attempted.

It was an exciting time for Caldecott, both on the road and at the fair; materials for his pencil were everywhere, and for three days there was little rest.

CATTLE FAIR AT CARHAIX.

Carhaix being in the centre of Brittany, far remote from railways, had special attractions in the variety of character and costume. Here, weak in health as Caldecott then was, he stood and worked all day, being especially interested in the trotting out and sale of horses. Turning to our diary :—

"The horse fair was held in a large square or *place.* Under the trees was a crowd of men and women in the dust and heat ; horses, cattle, pigs and dogs, in confused movement; with much drinking and shouting at the booths which lined one side of the enclosure."

A TYPICAL BRETON.

A BRETONNE.

It was in this year (1878) that he made some extra-ordinarily rapid sketches in colour with the brush direct, without a touch of the pencil or anything to guide him on the paper. Few sketches of this kind exist, excepting rough notes in books not intended for publication. In the evening the figures in the streets and at the inns had to be noted down.

The next day, which Caldecott called "a rest," was devoted to visiting two farms in the neigh-bourhood, seeing as much as possible of the in-teriors of the old houses near Carhaix, with their carved bedsteads, cabinets and clocks, old brass-work and embroideries. It was a rather anxious time for his travelling companion, for there was no restraining Caldecott with such material before him, and he was overworked.

It was in this district that he made one of his most successful sketches ; a typical Breton (p. 177), in ancient costume with long hair and

knee breeches; a figure rarely met with in these
days.

In the south-west corner of Brittany, a few miles
south of Quimperlé, at a point where the river
spreads out into a narrow estuary four miles
from the sea, is the primitive little village called
appropriately Pont Aven.

Caldecott was much amused, and scandalised at
the aspect of the village on our arrival one afternoon; a scene which he thus records on a letter,
and afterwards drew for *Breton Folk.*

Writing from Pont Aven and recounting "the
places which we have visited, done, sketched,
interviewed and memorandumed"—he adds :—

A CAP OF FINISTERRE.

"On this journey I have seen more pleasing types of Bretons (and Bretonnes, especially) than in my former rambles in the Côtes du Nord; but there is generally something wrong about each hotel. This particular inn is comfortable. Seven Americans, two or three of them ladies, and about four French people dined with us, mostly of the artist persuasion.

"The village and the river sides, the meadows and the valleys reek with artists. A large gang pensions at another inn here.

"On approaching Pont Aven the traveller notices a curious noise rising from the ground and from the woods around him. It is the flicking of the paint brushes on the canvasses of the hardworking painters who come into view seated in leafy nooks and shady corners. These artists go not far from the town where is cider, billiards and tobacco."

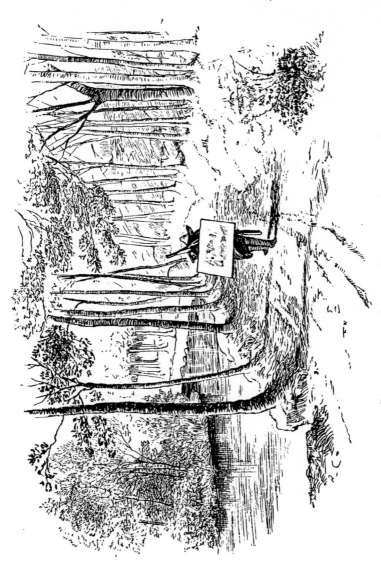

RETURNING FROM LABOUR—PONT AVEN, 1878.

One of the best of Caldecott's sketches here
was " Returning from Labour," a quiet spot on the
banks of the Aven where he made several studies.

" Here we feel inclined for the first time to stay
and sketch, wandering along the coast to the fishing
villages, and visiting farms and homesteads."

From another inn, in an " out of the way " part
of Finisterre, he writes :—

" The Hotel du Midi where we put up is conducted in a simple manner ; ladies would not like
its arrangements. Several inhabitants, and a visitor
or two, dine at the table d'hôte, but all are unable
to carve a duck excepting the English visitor, who
is accordingly put down as a cook."

Many works, such as the frieze of a horse fair
(p. 137), models in terra cotta and paintings, were
the outcome of the Brittany journeys in 1874
and 1878; but Caldecott did not give himself a
chance to do what he wished in France ; other
work crowded upon him in 1878, and before he
had time to finish the sketches for *Breton Folk*,
he had to return to London to complete drawings
for his *Picture Books*, and other work in hand for
the *Graphic* newspaper.

In a letter from London, received at the Abbey
of St. Jacut in Brittany on the 29th August, 1878,
he says :—

A BRETON.

" I have not been able to settle well down
to work yet. Sitting about on hotel benches for
a month with Mr. Blackburn is unhinging. * * *
" I fancied somehow that, after the wild career of
dissipation in other parts of Brittany, he might
find the calm of a cloister insufficiently exciting,
and consequently might drag you round to more
lively places. I am glad that I am wrong."

The drawings of the "Family Horse," (of "Cleopatra" on page 165,) the sketch in Woburn Park, and several others, were made when on a visit in the neighbourhood in October 1878. A letter referring to his visit to Woburn says :—" On the last evening of Mr. Caldecott's visit here, he was sitting at the dining-room table with the two little

" A FAMILY HORSE."

boys on his knees, and the rest of the family standing round him. We asked him to draw us each something, and he made us choose our own subjects. The sketch of himself riding in the park is one of them ; it amused him very much to see the deer standing gazing at us."

At another time there comes a coloured birthday

SKETCH IN WOBURN PARK

card to a child in London who was fond of flowers ;
a dark red carnation the size of life, presented by

A CARNATION.

a Lilliputian figure in old-fashioned green coat, with
white frill and periwig.

Side by side with Caldecott's missives to little
children might be printed many a kindly letter to a

young author who had sent him manuscripts to
read. These letters had to be read and answered
always in the evenings. A long letter of this
kind was written to a lady at Didsbury, near
Manchester, in 1878, from which the following
extracts are taken [1]:—

"DEAR MISS M.,—Your packet reached me safely, and as I call
to mind very readily my feelings in times gone by, after I had
posted a piece of literary or artistic composition to some friend
acquainted with the dread editor of some magazine, or even to the
dread editor himself, I think it only your due that I should write
to you without delay about the sketches of country life which you
have kindly allowed me to read, and my opinion of which you
flatter me by desiring to know. You asked me for my candid
opinion; in these cases I always try to be candid. . . . I think
that your papers are, as they stand, hardly interesting enough for
the mass of readers, though to me they draw out pictures which
please, and also revive old associations. . . .
Their fault, however, if I may speak of faults, is not so much in
subject as in style. You have chosen simple subjects, in which is
no harm of course; but simple subjects in all kinds of art require
a masterly hand to delineate them. The slightest awkwardness of
execution is noticed, and mars the simplicity of the whole. When
a thrilling story is told, or a very interesting and novel operation
described, faults of style are overlooked during the excitement of
hearing or reading. Is it not so? . . .   "R. C."

In another letter some remarks on the misuse of

---

[1] This letter was printed in the *Manchester City News*, 20 February, 1886.

old English words (a subject on which he says, " I
am very ignorant ") are worth recording.

"As regards the misuse of certain words, I
consult the authorities when a doubt crosses my
mind, and I find with sorrow, in which I am joined
by other anxious spirits, that the English language
is being ruined, chiefly by journalists, English and
American. Words of good old nervous meaning,
because common, are discarded for words of less
force but finer sound, borrowed from other tongues.
The use of these new words is often a difficulty to
all but classical scholars, for the pronunciation, the
accent, the quantities, are varied even amongst
equally educated people.

"On the introduction of a new word there is
always a halo of pedantry about it. Some admire
the halo and adopt the word. The journalists
cuddle it. The readers ask what it means, think it
sounds rather fine—perhaps genteel—throw over
the humble friend who has done them and their
conservative forefathers such good service.

"The poor ill-used old fellow of a word then only
finds friends amongst the lowly and the loyal ; and
if in course of time the usurping word, as he rolls
by in his carriage and footmen, hears the former
wearer of his honours come out from the passing
pedestrians, he curls his proud lip, pulls up his
haughty collar, distends his Grecian nose, and

wonders where vulgar people will go to—albeit this vulgar word is better born, and has a higher instep than the carriage word."

In the late Autumn of 1878 Caldecott is again in the south of France, sending home letters—one with a portrait of himself (back view), seated next to a young lady, " whose father is rather deaf."

*Hôtel Gray et d'Albion
Cannes,
15 Nov. 1878.*

" I have come here," he says, " in order that rheumatism may forget me and not recognise me on return to Albion's shores.   *   *   *

" I open my bag and take out your letter of 20th November, 1877, which has been ready at hand for reply ever since I received it with a welcome. Letters ought always to be replied to within the twelve months."

AT MENTONE.

CHAPTER XII.

AT MENTONE, ETC.

FROM the Riviera in 1879 came the following pictures in letters to friends.

" This hotel is indeed a calm spot, but the food is good, and I have a pleasant little room or two, where I can work comfortably. I know the inhabitant of one villa here, an American ; and I think there are two people whom I know in an hotel, so when I feel very lonely I shall hunt them up. There is much snow on the rocky hills near the

town, and the weather is rather cold, but the aspect
of everything around (nearly) is very fine and
worth coming to see."

In another letter he sends the following sketch of
himself at table in the vast *salle à manger* of the
hotel.[1]

"SPLENDIDE HOTEL, MENTON,
"*11th January,* 1879.

"DEAR ——,—The above view will give you a
more correct idea of the *splendour* of this hotel than
a page of writing, I think, could possibly do. It
represents our *table d'hôte* last night. I fled yesterday from Cannes, which—although called a very

---

[1] The portrait of Caldecott at the beginning of this volume, is from a
photograph taken at Cannes in January, 1879.

quiet place by most visitors—I found to be too lively
for one who has much work to do and a desire
to do it."

      *   *   *   *

Much drawing was accomplished in the spring of
this year, both abroad, and on return to London.
The success of his first Picture Books (on which he
writes, "I get a small, small royalty") was beyond all
expectation, and the *Elegy of a Mad Dog* was now
in progress.

Writing on the 20th June, in the wet summer of
1879, from 5, Langham Chambers, Portland Place (a
studio that he had taken temporarily from an artist
friend, Mr. W. J. Hennessy), he heads the letter

"Not such Disagreeable Weather after all—some People Think."

From *Punch*, August 2nd, 1879.

with the sketch on page 192, which is interesting as
the first idea for the drawing which appeared in
Punch on the 2nd August, 1879, reproduced on the
preceding page by permission of the proprietors.

A PIG OF BRITTANY (TERRA-COTTA).
The Property of Mr. Armstrong.

The illustration on the opposite page is an
example of Caldecott in a style which will be new
to most readers. The book plate was drawn for
an old and intimate friend in Manchester, and it

is curious to note how closely the style of the
family crest is followed in its various details.   If

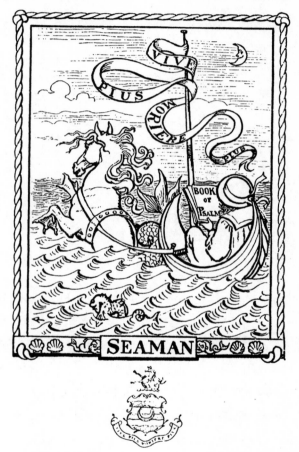

it were not for certain satirical touches this
ingenious design might easily pass for the work of

other hands ; the touch and treatment have little
in common with Caldecott as he is known ; but

the artistic completeness of the little book plate
is another evidence of his power as a designer.

In September Caldecott modelled some birds,
forming part of the capitals of pillars for Sir Frederick
Leighton's ' Arab Hall ' in his house at Kensington.
They were done for the architect, Mr. G. Aitchison,
A.R.A. Besides these he was at work on other
modelling ; one subject (the outcome of his Brittany
travels) is given on page 194.

In 1879 he took a small house, with an old-fashioned garden, at Kemsing, near Sevenoaks. This was his first country home, "an out-of-the-way place," as he expressed it, "but exactly right for me." Here, surrounded by his four-footed friends, he could indulge his liking and love for the country.

Writing to a young friend on the 13th October, he sends the following :—

"I am just now obliged to decline invitations to go and be merry with friends at a distance, because I am now living in this quiet, out-of-the-way village in order to make some studies of animals—to wit, horses, dogs, and other human beings—which I wish to use for the works that I shall be busy with during the coming winter.

"I have a mare—dark chestnut—who goes very well in harness, and is very pleasant to ride; and a little puppy—a comical young dachshund. My man calls the mare 'Peri,' so I call the puppy Lalla Rookh."

In a letter to his friend Mr. Locker-Lampson, written about this time, in 1880, he expresses surprise at not hearing from America respecting certain drawings by Miss Kate Greenaway and himself, which had been sent across the Atlantic to be engraved on wood. "I wonder why?" he says —[The rest is reproduced opposite].

Caldecott was soon found out in his country home, his wide reputation as an illustrator bringing him ever-increasing work, some "not very profitable."

Davis — the american en-
graver — has not written.
with the drawings & proof-
of blocks.   I will arouse him.

As he is — I fear.

As he ought
to be — I
am sure.

Yours faithfully
R. Caldecott

At this time he was taxing his energies to the utmost, working a long morning always indoors, and afterwards making studies in the garden or in the country, the evening occupied by reading and correspondence.

But he found time always—and until the end—to remember and to write to his old and dear friends. One more extract (the last in this book) from a letter from Venice, to an invalid friend in Manchester in 1880 :—

"I am sorry to hear that you are so lame," he says. "I wish you had been with us in Venice— the going to and fro in gondolas would have suited you well. Easy, smooth, and soul-subduing—especially by moonlight and when the ear is filled with the rich notes of a very uncommon gondolier's voice and the twanging of a sentimental traveller's lute.

"On the 18th of March we were married at a small church in Kent—my best man drove me in a dog-cart. I sold him my mare on the way, and she came to sad grief with him!"

SKETCH OF "WYBOURNES," KEMSING, NEAR SEVENOAKS.

The letters after this date refer to a period in Caldecott's art which must be considered at a future time. Only two remembrances of his later years shall be recorded now; one of him at Kemsing,

seated in his old-fashioned garden on a fine
summer's afternoon (after hard work from nine
till two) surrounded by his friends and four-footed
playmates—a garden where the birds, and even
the flowers, lived unrestrained.

> " Where woodbines wander, and the wallflower pushes
>   Its way alone ;
> And where, in wafts of fragrance, sweetbriar-bushes
>   Make themselves known.
> With banks of violets for southern breezes
>   To seek and find,
> And trellis'd jessamine that trembles in
>   The summer wind.
> Where clove-carnations overgrow the places
>   Where they were set,
> And, mist-like, in the intervening spaces
>   Creeps mignonette."

The other and a later remembrance of Caldecott
is at a gathering of friends in Victoria Street,
Westminster, in January, 1885, when—to a good
old English tune—the "lasses and lads," out of
his *Picture Book*, danced before him, and the
fiddler, in the costume of the time, "played it
wrong."

A New Year's Greeting to a Friend.

CHAPTER XIII.

CONCLUSION.

It will be seen in the preceding pages that it
was the privilege of the writer to know Caldecott
intimately before he had made a name, when his
heart and hands were free, so to speak ; when he
was untrammelled by much sense of responsibility,
or by the necessity of keeping up a reputation,
and when every day, almost, recorded some new
experiment or achievement in his art. Let it
be stated here that not at that time, nor ever

afterwards in the writer's hearing, was a word said
against Caldecott. With a somewhat wide and
exceptional experience of the personality of artists,
it can be said with truth that Caldecott was "a
man of whom all spoke well." His presence then,
as in later years, seemed to dispel all jealousies,
if they ever existed, and to scatter evil spirits if
they ever approached him. No wonder—for was
he not the very embodiment of sweetness, simple-
mindedness, generosity, and honour ?

From the sketch on page 1 of this book, made
in the smoke of Manchester, to the "New Year's
Greeting" on p. 203, the same happy, joyous
spirit is evident ; and so, to those who knew him,
he remained to the end.

As this memoir has to do with Caldecott's earlier
career, and particularly with his work in black
and white, the artistic value of his illustrations in
colour, especially in his *Picture Books*, can only
be hinted at here.

Caldecott's Picture Books are known all over the
world ; they have been widely discussed and
criticised, and they form undoubtedly the best

monument to his memory. But it may be found
that some of the best work he ever did (the
work least open to criticism) was in 1874 and
1875, before these books were begun ; and that the
material here collected will aid in forming a better
estimate of Caldecott as an artist.

In March, 1883, there appeared a little oblong
Sketch Book with canvas cover, full of original and
delightful illustrations, many in colour, engraved and
printed by Edmund Evans. This book is not
very widely known, but there are drawings in it of
great personal interest, now that the artist's hand
is still. The *Sketch Book* suggests many thoughts
and calls up many associations to those who knew
him.

In 1883 he illustrated *Æsop's Fables* with " Modern Instances " (referred to on page 94).

The kind of work that Caldecott liked best,
and of which he would have been an artistic and
delightful exponent had circumstances permitted, is
indicated in the design at the head of the preface
to this volume; it was drawn on brown paper,
probably for a wood carving in relief, for the central

panel of a mantelpiece. This sketch is selected from several designs of a similar kind.

In purely journalistic work, for which his powers seemed eminently fitted, he was never at home, his heart was not in it. Neither on *Punch* nor on the *Graphic* newspaper, would he have engaged to work regularly. He would do anything on an emergency to aid a friend—or a foe, if he had known one—but neither health nor inclination led him in that direction. And yet Caldecott, of all contemporary artists, owed his wide popularity to the wood engraver, to the maker of colour blocks, and to the printing press. No artist before him had such chances of dispersing facsimiles of daintily coloured illustrations over the world. All this must be considered when his place in the century of artists is written.

Mr. Clough touches a true note in the following (from the *Manchester Quarterly*) :—

"If the art, tender and true as it is, be not of the highest, yet the artist is expressed in his work as perhaps few others have been. Nothing to be regretted—all of the clearest—an open-air, pure life—a clean soul. Wholesome as the England he loved so well. Manly, tolerant, and patient under suffering. None of the

friends he made did he let go.   No envy, malice, or uncharitable-
ness spoiled him ; no social flattery or fashionable success, made
him forget those he had known, in the early years."

Speaking generally of his friend Caldecott, whom
he had known intimately in later years, Mr. Locker-
Lampson (to whom we are indebted for the letters
and sketches on pages 191, 192, and 199), writes :—

"It seems to me that Caldecott's art was of a quality that
appears about once in a century.   It had delightful characteristics
most happily blended.   He had a delicate fancy, and his humour
was as racy as it was refined.   He had a keen sense of beauty,
and, to sum up all, he had *charm*.   His old-world youths and
maidens are perfect.   The men are so simple and so manly, the
maidens are so modest and so trustful : The latter remind one of
the country girl in that quaint old ballad,

> " ' He stopt and gave my cheek a pat,
>   He told a tender tale,
>   Then stole a kiss, but what of that ?
>   'Twas Willie of the Dale ! '

"Poor Caldecott !   His friends were much attached to him
He had feelings, and ideas, and manners, which made him
welcome in any society ; but alas, all was trammelled, not obscured,
by deplorably bad health."

These two criticisms—both coming from friends
of the artist, but from different points of view—are
worth setting side by side in a memoir.

A correspondent, writing from Manchester, sends
the following interesting letter respecting places

sketched by Caldecott in Cheshire and Shropshire and afterwards used in the illustrations in his books.

" During occasional rambles in this and the neighbouring county of Chester, more especially in the neighbourhood of Whitchurch, I have been interested in the identification of some few of the original scenes pictured by Mr. Caldecott in his several published drawings.   Thus :—

" Malpas Church, which occupies the summit or a gentle hill some six miles from Whitchurch, occurs frequently—as in a full page drawing in the *Graphic* newspaper for Christmas, 1883 ; in *Babes in the Wood*, p. 19 ; in *Baby Bunting*, p. 20 ; and in *The Fox Jumps over the Parson's Gate*, p. 5.

" The main street of Whitchurch is fairly pictured in the *Great Panjandrum*, p. 6, whilst the old porch of the Blue Bell portrayed on p. 28 of *Old Christmas* is identical with that of the Bell Inn at Lushingham, situated some two miles from Whitchurch on the way to Malpas.

" Besides these I recognise in the ' Old Stone-house, Lingborough Hall,' in *Lob Lie-by-the-Fire*, p. 5, an accurate line-for-line sketch of Barton Hall, an ancient moated mansion which until quite recently stood within the parish of Eccles, four miles from Manchester.

" Lastly, a comparison of the illustration on p. 95 of *Old Christmas*, with one in last year's volume of the *English Illustrated Magazine*, p. 466, shows that the picturesque nooks of Sussex, equally with those of Kent and Chester, yielded their quota to the busy pencil we know so well."

About the year 1879 Caldecott became acquainted with Mrs. Ewing, which led to his making many illustrations for her, such as the design for the cover of *Aunt Judy's Magazine*, and notably the

illustrations to that "book of books" for boys,
"*Jackanapes,*" and to "*Daddy Darwin's Dovecot,*"
and others.

Miss Gatty, in her memoir of Mrs. Ewing, says :—

"My sister was in London in June, 1879, and then made the
acquaintance of Mr. Caldecott, for whose illustrations she had
unbounded admiration. This introduction led us to ask him
(when *Jackanapes* was still simmering in Julie's brain) if he would
supply a coloured illustration for it. But as the tale was only
written a very short time before it appeared, and as the illustration
was wanted early and colours take long to print, Julie could not
send the story to be read, but asked Caldecott to draw her a
picture to fit one of the scenes in it. The one she suggested was
a fair-haired boy on a red-haired pony, thinking of one of her own
nephews, a skilful seven-year-old rider who was accustomed to
follow the hounds."

Looking back, but a few months only, at the
passing away of two such lives—the author of
"*Jackanapes*" and the illustrator of the "*Picture
Books*" (of whom it was well said lately, "they
have gone to Heaven together")—the loss seems
incalculable.

In the history of the century, the best and purest
books and the brightest pages ever placed before
children will be recorded between 1878 and 1885 ;
and no words would seem more in touch with the

lives and aims of these lamented artists than a concluding sentence in *Jackanapes*, that—their works are "a heritage of heroic example and noble obligation."

The grace and beauty, and wealth of imagination in Caldecott's work,—conspicuous to the end,— form a monument which few men in the history of illustrative art have raised for themselves.

Here may end fittingly the memoir of his earlier work. At a future time more may be written, and many delightful reminiscences recorded, of the years from the time of his marriage on the 18th March, 1880, to his lamented death at St. Augustine, in Florida, on the 12th February, 1886; when—in the sympathetic lines which appeared in *Punch* on the 27th February, 1886:—

> " All that flow of fun, and all
>   That fount of charm found in his fancy,
> Are stopped!   Yet will he hold us thrall
>   By his fine art's sweet necromancy,
> Children and seniors many a year ;
>   For long 'twill be ere a new-comer,
> Fireside or nursery holdeth dear
>   As him whose life ceased in its summer."

COMING SOON FROM FISHER PRESS
COVENTRY PATMORE
THE BOW IN THE CLOUD

At a time when marriage is under attack those concerned about the social consequences of its decline may wish to look again at the writings of the Victorian poet who made married love his main theme. Happily married three times, Patmore used his experience to develop a theory of marriage. His first two wives predeceased him; his third survived his death. His understanding of love is unlike Plato's, who rejects the body as unruly; or Dante's, whose beloved is always outside marriage and unattainable. Patmore knew that passion was always inherent in real men and women. What was needed was for it to be ordered in accordance with the eternal law, rather than disordered, as occurs when sexual relations occur outside the marriage bond. He observed that those who reject marriage were not more joyful than those who make marriage vows and keep them. This remains the case today, in spite of concerted attempts to persuade men and women that changing partners as whim dictates, without guilt or regret, leads to personal fulfilment which equates with happiness.

There are other reasons too for proclaiming Patmore the least "politically correct" of the great Victorians. For he shared Dr. Johnson's view that inequality and subordination were the source of all delight. It was the different, unequal nature of men and women which made the love between them, when duly ordered, the perfect representation of the love between God and the soul. In politics too Patmore defended another currently unfashionable view: that it was better for a nation to be governed by right reason rather than for all its citizens to be compelled to participate in misgoverning themselves. He saw that democratic majorities would often tyrannise their minorities, and require the State to impose their tastes and crush any dissent, rather than, as he would wish, encourage all citizens to aspire to individual excellence and virtue. For we who are presently faced with an expanding prison population, a catastrophic loss of virtue, and State interference in our private lives, Patmore's alternative vision, based on his keen observation of human nature and clear logic, deserves closer attention.

As well as being a poet, Patmore was a mathemetician, astronomer, successful farmer, connoisseur of precious stones and chemist (he always made the family fireworks himself!). Roger Scruton has encouraged a revival of interest in his writing on architecture and art; these important contributions are included in this collection as well his major writings on literature, politics, the relations between the sexes, religion and the moral life.

130 x198 mm
Wood-free paper £8.99   ISBN 1 874037 13 2

ALSO FROM FISHER PRESS

HUGH DORMER D.S.O.
WAR DIARY

With a facsimile of a leaf from his secret diary, maps, military sketch
plan, and a drawing by John Dormer, the artist brother of the author.

Nothing in World War II fiction captures the excitement and terror of SOE's clan-
destine operations so well as Hugh Dormer's authentic *Diary* of 15 months in 1943-
44. Although many other young Englishmen sacrificed their lives for the people of
France, few had the talent to describe the daring events both accurately for intelli-
gence purposes, and in a way which is of lasting literary value. Several years of training with the Irish Guards Armoured Division for the long-awaited D Day landing
made Hugh Dormer restless for action. In October 1942 he volunteered for subver-
sion work in German-occupied France, despite his strong English accent when speaking French. He was twice parachuted into France in 1943, leading small bands of
men to dynamite key components of industrial plants being operated for the German
military machine. The diary is a record of these attacks, much of it written in secret
at the time, and of his escapes through occupied France and over the Pyrenees. Yet it
is the clarity of his understanding of the war as nothing less than the defence of
Christian civilization, for which the martyrs in earlier times had also died, which
gives the *War Diary* its greatness. For while on the run in France he observes at close
hand what can happen when men and nations begin to lose the moral and spiritual
values which they have acquired over so many centuries. The results were horrific:
men betraying their neighbours, rejecting their children, sending their compatriots to
death camps; indiscriminate bloody reprisals; the forced labour of the young; above
all the paralysis of knowing what should be done, but failing to act out of cold fear. It
was to help the French believe once more that it was possible to be free of tyranny
and again act rightly and honourably that motivated Hugh Dormer. Readers will be
fully engaged in his internal struggle when he decides that, despite his D.SO. and the
offer of a leading role with SOE in Western France, his final contribution to French
liberation should be, not as a modern-day Scarlet Pimpernel, but as a soldier with his
beloved Irish guardsmen. The diary ends with his account of the D day landings, and
the armoured push into Normandy in which he was killed.

130 x198 mm 160 pages
Wood-free paper £7.99   ISBN 1 874037 11 6

**If you have difficulty in obtaining Fisher Press books from your local
bookshop you can order them direct from Post Office Box
41,Sevenoaks, Kent TN15 6YN. Telephone/Fax 01732 761830**